For Heaven's Sake

FOR HEAVEN'S SAKE

by
Peter Kreeft

THOMAS NELSON PUBLISHERS
Nashville • Camden • New York

Published in Nashville, Tennessee, by Thomas Nelson, Inc., and distributed in Canada by Lawson Falle, Ltd., Cambridge, Ontario.

Printed in the United States of America.

Unless otherwise noted, the Bible version used in the publication is THE NEW KING JAMES VERSION. Copyright © 1979, 1980, 1982, Thomas Nelson, Inc., Publishers.

Scripture quotations noted KJV are from the King James Version of the Bible.

Scripture quotations noted RSV are from the Revised Standard Version of the Bible, copyrighted 1946, 1952, © 1971, 1973 by the Division of Christian Education of the National Council of the Churches of Christ in the U.S.A. and used by permission.

Library of Congress Cataloging-in-publication Data

Kreeft, Peter.
  For heaven's sake.

  1. Virtue.   2. Virtues.   3. Beatitudes.   4. Deadly sins.   I. Title.
BV4630.K73   1986   179'.9   86-8773
IBN 0-8407-5494-9

For Edna
who already knows this
because she knows Him

virtue (n.) 1. Moral excellence; right living; goodness. 2. A particular type of moral excellence. 3. A good quality or feature. 4. Purity, chastity. 5. Effectiveness.

Virtue comes from the Latin word *virtus,* which meant *manliness,* or virility. Thus, as one wag notes, the word which used to mean a man's ability to impregnate a woman (meaning 5) came to mean a woman's ability not to be impregnated by a man (meaning 4).

CONTENTS

Can virtue be taught? That question of the fifth century before Christ looms gigantic again near the end of the twentieth century of the Christian era. Peter Kreeft, who perceives much about life and death, aspires to teach us about *virtues,* both classical and theological.

He does not aspire to teach us about *values,* praise be. As he puts it, "Values are like thoughts, like ghosts, undulating blobs of psychic energy." The positivistic sociologist would reduce our moral order to personal preferences called "values"; Professor Kreeft has taken arms against such reductionists.

The practical aim of this book is to help in the restoration of moral habits among the rising generation. Gustave Le Bon remarks that we folk of the twentieth century may be more moralistic than were medieval people, in the sense that we fret more about morality, but men and women of the Middle Ages had better moral habits. In medieval times, the seven cardinal virtues were known to everyone, while nowadays it is a rare university student who can name the seven.

In its classical signification, *virtue* means the power of anything to accomplish its specific function; a property capable of producing certain effects; strength, force, potency. Also the word *virtue* implies a mysterious energetic power, as in the gospel according to Mark: "Jesus, immediately knowing . . . that *virtue* had gone out of him, turned him about in the press, and said, Who touched my clothes?" (Mark 5:30 KJV, italics added).

Presently, *virtue* also signifies moral goodness; the practice of moral duties and the conformity of one's life to the moral law; uprightness; rectitude. It carries with it a strong suggestion of public leadership.

Peter Kreeft reminds us that "ethics without virtue is illusion." He is moved by the Christian perception that virtue is the fruit of faith. Therefore, he does not hesitate to draw the sword of faith and then sound the horn of virtue, rallying us (in the phrases of Pico della Mirandola) "to join battle as to the sound of a trumpet of war" on behalf of man's higher nature, defying the vegetative and sensual errors of our age. This book, *For Heaven's Sake,* is steeped in old virtues. It exhorts us to renew them.

Russell Kirk

Is Virtue Out-of-date?

"**A** book about virtues and vices? How quaint! How out-of-date!" A civilization with such a notion of virtues and vices will soon be quaint and out-of-date.

In that past civilization that most nearly resembles our own, late Rome, the barbarians at the gates were only the external reflection of the barbarity within. So with us: The nuclear holocaust that threatens us from without is only the mirror image of the holocaust of the heart.

When you are edging closer and closer to the abyss, the most progressive direction is backwards. Our nuclear abyss is now so close and so well-known that no one can ignore it. There are only two roads that lead back from the edge. One of these roads is closed forever. It is the road of ignorance, ignorance of the facts about how to make nuclear bombs. The other road is the road of knowledge, knowledge of moral virtue that would make it unthinkable ever to use them. That road, the subject of this book, is still open. Our cult of novelty has brought us to the brink of suicide. Modern Western man cultivates risk and revolution. He scorns the traditional, the tried and true. That is one of the reasons the supreme novelty of nuclear holocaust looms so hideously possible on our horizon.

Walker Percy says there is one thing that secretly terrifies us even more than life with a nuclear war: life with no nuclear war.

A friend of mine recently taught a course to some bright prep school students on the problem of nuclear war. The students were highly motivated and fascinated with the question. At the end of the course most of them had come to believe that there will *not* be a nuclear war. What do you think their reaction was? Joy? Relief? No. Shock, an empty look, and a deeper and subtler terror than the fear of death, the terror not at physical nothingness but at spiritual nothingness. "What do we do now?" The existential vacuum!

The feeling must have been like that of the early Seventh Day Adventists whose lives had been geared to the world's ending on a certain date and when the date passed, found themselves still here. What now?

It is a simple question but an awful one. What now? For behind its horizon looms a face more hideous even than that of the mushroom cloud, the face of The Nothing.

What can fill The Nothing? What is its opposite, its opponent, its conqueror?

Being human fills The Nothing. Getting on with the business of life answers the question, What now?

But what *is* it to be human? What *is* the business of life? We must succeed at our primary career, which is not business, or construction work, or sales, or teaching, or even motherhood, but becoming a complete human being. But what is that?

There used to be maps, diagrams, pictures of a complete human being. A very large part of those old maps were about virtues and vices, good and bad qualities of character and life. But the old maps have fallen into disuse.

In this book I try to perform the radical task of blowing some dust off the old maps, so that you can make the astonishing discovery that the old maps still work and that you can't tell truth by the clock. In other words, this book is basic moral teaching, the kind of thing you could expect from run-of-the-mill philosophers as a matter of course for the last few millennia but which has become increasingly scarce in our time. C. S. Lewis remarked that he wrote the books he wished someone else had written but didn't. I feel the same.

The first part of this book, chapters one through three, is about virtue for survival on earth, virtue for Western civilization. The second part is about virtue as such, virtue for individuals. Many readers will think the first part is more important, but I disagree, for two reasons. First, the only way to a good society is through good individuals. As Confucius said:

> If there is harmony in the heart, there will be harmony in the family.
> If there is harmony in the family, there will be harmony in the nation.
> If there is harmony in the nation, there will be harmony in the world.

Second, individuals are infinitely more important than civilizations because they are immortal. When all civilizations are dead, when even the stars blink out billions of years from now, every one of us will still exist, in eternal joy or eternal misery. And that is the only issue that matters infinitely: Quo vadis?

PART I

Missing: A Virtuous People

CHAPTER ONE

A Civilization at Risk:
Whatever Became of Virtue?

A prominent Christian businessman is exposed as a crook and a bigamist. A historic Christian denomination goes on record as favoring a woman's right to abortion. The second fact is even more shocking and serious than the first.

Why?

A brilliant Christian writer and pastor leaves his wife and children and runs off with another woman. Then he writes a book justifying it. The second fact is more shocking than the first.

Why?

Nearly as many of the marriages of Christians end in divorce as those of non-Christians. Most Christian denominations permit divorce, though Christ did not. The second fact is more shocking than the first.

Why?

THE OUTLAWING OF VIRTUE

In each of the above cases, the first statement shows only the perennial fact of hypocrisy, of not practicing what one preaches or believes. But the second statements are something altogether new. They represent a changing of the rules that makes hypocrisy impossible!

Matthew Arnold defined hypocrisy as a "tribute that vice pays to virtue." With that tribute no longer paid, we no longer need virtue. The first of each set of facts above shows a lack of virtue; the second shows a lack of *knowledge* of virtue. This is new. Christians, like other sinners, have always been susceptible to vice, but today we no longer seem to know what vice and virtue are.

The solution to the first perennial problem is repentance and divine grace, something a book cannot help much with. But the solution to the second problem is knowledge, and there a book can help.

Help is desperately needed exactly now. For exactly at the time when the fatal knowledge of how to destroy the entire human race has fallen forever into our hands, the knowledge of morality has fallen out. Exactly when the vehicle of our history has gotten a souped-up engine, we have lost the road map. Exactly when our toys have grown up with us from bows and arrows to thermonuclear bombs, we have become moral infants.

If a child's moral growth does not keep pace with his physical growth, there may soon be no child. Could this explain why the most common age for suicide today is adolescence? The human race is now in its adolescence and standing on the edge of a cliff.

The most terrifying things (other than demons) ever to appear on our planet—thermonuclear bombs—have done a wonderful thing, a thing all the moralists, preachers, prophets, saints, and sages in history could not do: They have made the practice of virtue a necessity, not a luxury. In W. H. Auden's simple and perfect formula, "We must love one another or die."

However, to practice morality, we must first know it. To be men and women of virtue, not vice, we must know what *virtue* and *vice* mean.

THE FREAK OF WESTERN CIVILIZATION

Our modern Western civilization is a freak because it is radically different from every other civilization that has ever appeared on this planet. How? Most obviously in its technology. But more deeply, in the spiritual origin of its technology, which is a new philosophy, a new answer to the most important of all questions: Why was I born? Why am I living? In what should I invest my hopes, my dreams, my longing and living and loving? What are the best things in life? What is the *summum bonum,* or greatest good?

To that perennial last question Francis Bacon formulated the new answer: "Man's conquest of nature." C. S. Lewis wrote a prophetic little masterpiece of a book about what happens when this new philosophy is combined with the loss of the knowledge of morality and virtue. The title says it neatly, *The Abolition of Man.*

The term *man* in the phrase "man's conquest of nature" is a sexually chauvinistic term, not because all use of the traditional generic *man* is, but because we have a civilization that is in the midst of what Karl Stern called (in another prophetic title) *The Flight from Woman.* We extol action over contemplation, doing over being, analysis over intuition, problems over mysteries, success over contentment, conquering over nurturing, the quick fix over lifelong commitment, the prostitute over the mother.

Long ago, Aristotle taught that there are three reasons for seeking knowledge. The most important one is truth, the next is moral action, and the last and least important is power, or the ability to make things: technique, technology, know-how. Bacon and modernity have turned Aristotle upside down.

We have sown the wind and reaped the whirlwind. This generation, we and our children, not some vague, safely distant future generation, now stand at the reckoning point. The most important decision in history is ours to make. We cannot return to technological ignorance, nor should we want to. But we can return to the knowledge of morality (and we should at least want to)—the knowledge that makes us the kind of people who can use these terrible new powers responsibly. What kind of people would that be? One with character and with virtue, two words which are seriously out of fashion, even embarrassing, today. That is precisely our problem.

I have never read any three sentences that go more deeply to the heart of our civilization and its distinctiveness than these from *The Abolition of Man:*

> There is something which unites magic and applied science [technology] while separating them from the "wisdom" of earlier ages. For the wise men of old, the cardinal problem of human life was how to conform the soul to objective reality, and the solution was wisdom, self-discipline, and virtue. For the modern, the cardinal problem is how to conform reality to the wishes of man, and the solution is a technique.[1]

TWO WORLD VIEWS

With this new practical philosophy of the conquest of nature comes a new theoretical philosophy that objective reality *is* only nature, that nature is all there is. This is Naturalism, the reduction of objective reality to matter, time, space, and motion.

The alternative to this philosophy is Supernaturalism, the belief that objective reality includes also something more than nature, something like God. If "objective reality" means God, then we had better conform to Him, and it is silly to try to make Him conform to us. But if "objective reality" means only nature, then we can conquer it, and it is silly to conform to it.

The common principle of both philosophies is that the inferior should conform to the superior, not vice versa. The premodern practical philosophy, or life-view, flowed from the premodern theoretical philosophy, or world-view: There is a God; therefore conform to Him. The modern life-view flows from the modern world-view: There is no God; therefore we play God to the world (see Figure 1). Both philosophies are consistent, but one of the two must be wrong, disastrously wrong.

Until recently, our civilization could still feel optimistic about its

TWO WORLD VIEWS

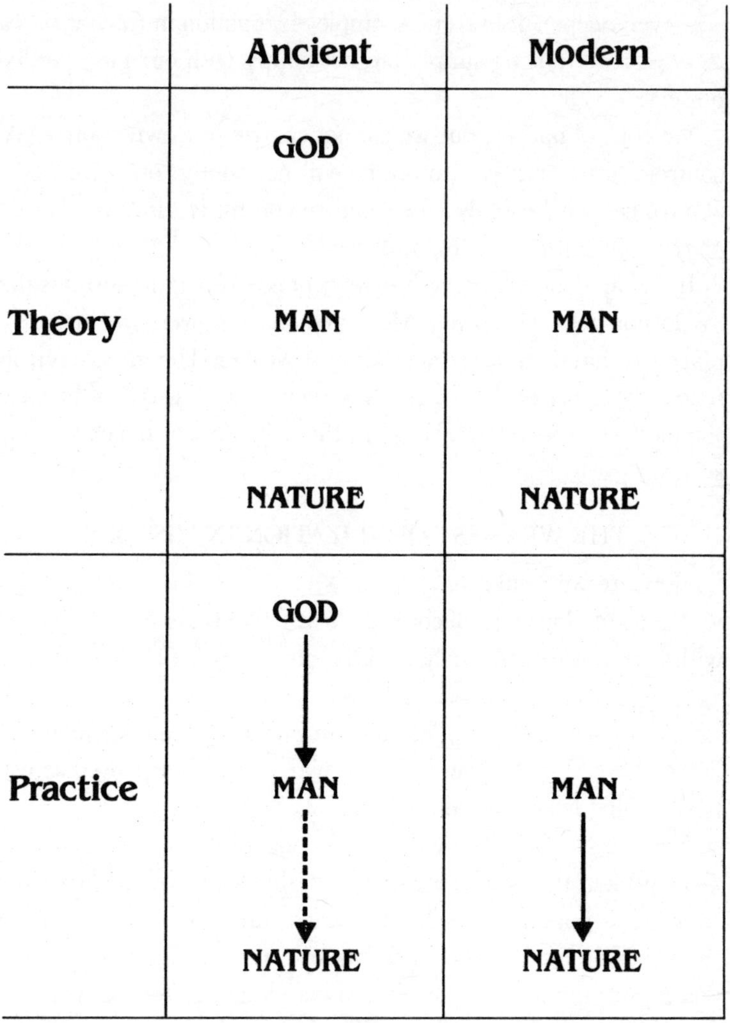

	Ancient	Modern
Theory	GOD MAN NATURE	MAN NATURE
Practice	GOD ↓ MAN ↓ NATURE	MAN ↓ NATURE

Figure 1

new ideal and its associated myth of universal and necessary progress. There are two reasons why the optimism is dying. One is, of course, the fear of collective thermonuclear suicide, but the other cuts even deeper. It is Freud's simple observation in *Civilization and Its Discontents* that we simply are not happy with our new, godlike powers.

We control nature, but we cannot control our own control. We control nature, but we cannot or will not control ourselves. Self-control is "out" exactly when nature-control is "in," that is, exactly when self-control is most needed.

If we can conquer everything except ourselves, the result is that *we* do not hold the power. More and more power over nature is placed in hands that are weaker and weaker. Heredity, environment, the spirit of the times, "the inevitable dialectic of history," the media—*something* is always in the driver's seat instead of ourselves.

THE WEAKEST CIVILIZATION IN HISTORY

How are we weak?

Not technologically, of course. We are like King Midas, swollen with new powers and riches, although at a price: Everything we touch has gone dead and cold.

Not intellectually. We learn more and more, though it means less and less. We are overwhelmed with knowledge as well as with power. Our heads are about to burst. Some do.

Nor are we morally weaker. I do not think we are necessarily more wicked than our ancestors, overall. True, we are less courageous, less honest, less self-disciplined, and obviously less chaste than they were. But they were more cruel, intolerant, snobbish, and inhumane than we are. They were better at the hard virtues; we are better at the soft virtues. The balance is fairly even, I think.

But though we are not weaker in morality, we are weaker in the *knowledge* of morality. We are stronger in the knowledge of nature, but weaker in the knowledge of goodness. We know more about what is less than ourselves but less about what is more than ourselves. When we act morally, we are better than our philosophy. Our ancestors were worse than theirs. Their problem was not living up to their principles. Ours is not having any.

We have lost objective moral law for the first time in history. The philosophies of moral positivism (meaning that morality is posited or made by man) and of moral relativism and subjectivism have become for the first time not a heresy for rebels but the reigning orthodoxy of the intellectual establishment. University faculty and media personnel overwhelmingly reject belief in the notion of universal and objective moral values.

Yet our civilization, especially the two groups just mentioned, *talk* a good game of ethics. Ethical *discussion* has grown into the gap left by a dying ethical *vision*. It is the kind of discussion Saint Paul described as "ever learning and never coming to a knowledge of the truth." (Perhaps he had a prophetic vision of our modern TV talk shows!) It is intellectual Ping-Pong, sharing views rather than seeking truth. For how can we seek something we do not believe in? The notions that there is objective truth in the realm of morality and that an open mind is therefore not an end in itself but a means to the end of finding truth are labeled "simplistic" by the intellectual establishment when, in fact, they are simple sanity and common sense. (As G. K. Chesteron says, an open mind is like an open mouth: useful only to close down on something solid.)

In an age of anything goes, virtue is a revolutionary thing. In an age of rebellion, authority is the radical idea. In an age of pell-mell "progress" to annihilation, tradition is the hero on the white horse.

WE LIVE IN TWO WORLDS

We have gotten to the point where moral values have become both privatized and collectivized. On the one hand, the modern mind has fallen victim to what C. S. Lewis calls "the poison of subjectivism": the idea that morality is manmade, private, subjective, a matter of feeling, a subdivision of psychology. "I feel" replaces "I believe."

On the other hand, sociology has socialized and collectivized morality; consensus determines rightness or wrongness, and democracy becomes our religion; *vox populi vox dei* ("the voice of the people is the voice of God"). These two developments, privatism and collectivism, may seem contradictory, but they have happened simultaneously in the modern West.

Their effect is that we live in two separate worlds. Our feeling life, our inner world of values (no longer real *goods*), is set against the outer world of behavior, a world governed by social mores (no longer real *morals*). Values are like thoughts, like ghosts, undulating blobs of psychic energy. Mores are like brute facts, ways people do in fact behave, not ways they *ought* to. We are like ghosts in machines.

What happens if we bring together these two halves of our alienated world? What happens when we realize that our subjective consciousness is a prophet of objective reality? What happens when we realize that objective reality includes not just brute facts but also goods, not only *ises* but also *oughts,* not only the fact that society *does* do such-and-such, but also the fact that society *ought* to do so-and-so?

When this meeting of the two hemispheres of our cracked world takes place, it is like a homecoming between alienated lovers. A shudder reaches us, deep and breathtaking. We have run away from that shudder for centuries. Martin Buber writes:

At times the man, shuddering at the alienation between the *I* and the world, comes to reflect that something is to be done. . . . And thought, ready with its service and its art, paints with its well-known speed one—no, two—rows of pictures, on the right wall and on the left. On the one there is . . . the universe. The tiny earth plunges from the whirling stars, tiny man from the teeming earth, and now history bears him further through the ages, to rebuild persistently the ant-hill of the cultures which history crushes underfoot. . . . On the other wall there takes place the soul. A spinner is spinning the orbits of all stars and the life of all creation and the history of the universe; everything is woven of one thread, and is no longer called stars and creation and universe, but sensations and imaginings, or even experiences, and conditions of the soul. . . .

Thenceforth, if ever the man shudders at the alienation, and the world strikes terror in his heart, he looks up (to right or left, just as it may chance) and sees a picture. There he sees that the *I* is embedded in the world and that there is really no *I* at all—so the world can do nothing to the *I*, and he is put at ease; or he sees that the world is embedded in the *I*, and that there is really no world at all—so the world can do nothing to the *I*, and he is put at ease. . . .

But a moment comes, and it is near, when the shuddering man looks up and sees both pictures in a flash together. And a deeper shudder seizes him.[2]

MORAL UNEDUCATION: VALUES CLARIFICATION

Two recent developments are an index of our value-ignorance: Values clarification is "in," and proverbs are "out." What does this mean?

Proverbs are the summaries of the accumulated practical wisdom of the past, the experience of our ancestors. They are moral truths, half-truths sometimes, but truths. They describe real virtues. But we no longer believe in real virtues. Therefore we do not believe in proverbs. We believe instead in discussion, in moral Ping-Pong, in "values clarification."

Values clarification is essentially the following. Facilitators (no longer teachers, for there is no longer anything true to teach) encourage students to state and clarify their own personal values by asking questions. This sounds like Socrates so far, but wait.

These questions are never about the roots or grounds of values, about *principles*. Instead, they are about feelings and reasonings, *calculations* (e.g., if you were in a lifeboat with four people and there were only enough food for two to survive, what would you do?). Such questions do not touch the roots of morality. They never ask questions about virtues and vices, about character, but ask only about what you would do, or rather what you would feel comfortable doing. A choice to have or not to have an abortion is put to the student in the same way, with the same tone, as a choice between Christmas presents or foods. And tone is a factor that children are very sensitive to.

The facilitator theoretically does not lead the students in any way. The one moral absolute in values clarification is that there are no moral absolutes, and the only thing forbidden is for the facilitator to suggest that his or her beliefs are true, or even to suggest that there is objective truth in the realm of values, for that would mean that some of the students are wrong, and that would be judgmental, the only sin. In fact, the very procedure itself teaches a nearly irresistible lesson: Values are all up for grabs, are matters of individual or social taste; no one has the right to teach another here; values are "my" values or "your" values, never simply true values; values, in short, are not facts but feelings.

Many theorists in the movement will admit explicitly that the deliberate purpose of values clarification in schools is a social revolution to undermine the authority of parents whose values are felt to be regressive and repressive and thus to pave the way for social change. These traditional values are never attacked rationally, directly, and honestly, whether because the theorists no longer believe in the value of honesty or of reason or, more likely, because they cannily foresee that thereby they will suffer a devastating defeat. Values clarification is not an angry stroke of a sword; it is a sly, knowing wink. After all, what can parents without Ph.D.'s in sociology possibly know?

A LITTLE MORALITY IS A DANGEROUS THING

There is a brilliant strategy behind teaching ethics without virtues and vices. This strategy is not an organized or conscious movement or conspiracy, at least not by human beings. But it is there and it has the effect of an *inoculation*. We build up an immunity to the real thing, just as a weak dose of a disease germ such as cowpox builds up an immunity to the stronger disease of smallpox.

The immunity usually takes the form of thinking we already have the real thing and therefore scorning those who do, who explicitly or implicitly criticize popular morality (the inoculation). It uses a powerful tool; the word *fanatic*. There is absolutely no word in our language which ostracizes a person from today's intellectual establishment more than this word, especially when combined with another dirty word to produce the supreme insult, "religious fanatic." Of course, no distinction is made between religious fanaticism and traditional religious belief as such.

If you confess at a fashionable cocktail party that you personally love to play with porcupines, or plan to sell CIA secrets to the Communists, or that you are considering becoming a Palestinian terrorist, you will find a buzzing, fascinated crowd around you, eager to listen. But if you confess that you believe that Jesus is God, that He died to save us from sin, or that there really are a Heaven and a Hell, you will very soon be talking to empty air, with a distinct chill in it.

This is why great sinners, who are not inoculated with a little morality, become great saints more often than "respectable," inoculated people do. Ethics without virtue is "a little morality." It is like religion without God, at least the living God. Dealing with the living God is a little like a nuclear war: it can upset your whole day.

But so can atheism. We dislike being upset by any extreme. Many people have been lured to theism by the honest and unendurable despair of the great atheists like Nietzsche, Camus, and Sartre. But the popular religion of a vague divine sense or "The Force," as in *Star Wars,* is a wonderful consolation against both the terror of ultimate nothingness and the equal terror of ultimate goodness.

Those who are sick, said Jesus, know they have need of a physician, but not those who are well (or think they are). Those who have no ethics, the Machiavellians, are ripe for conversion, as were Saints Augustine, Francis, and Ignatius, as well as Chuck Colson. Those who seem to have ethics but actually do not are comfortably ensconced in illusion.

Ethics without virtue is illusion. What is the highest purpose of ethics? It is to make people good, that is, virtuous. Without a road map of the virtues and vices, how likely is it that we will find our way home, especially if we are lost? And the one thing nearly everyone admits is that modern man is lost.

Meanwhile, while ethics languish, *discussion* of ethics flourishes. One of the most popular elective courses in high schools and colleges is ethics. But the kind of ethics that is usually taught is ethics without bite, without substance, without power, for ethics without a vision of what a good man or woman is, without virtues and vices, concentrates on doing instead of being, just as our whole modern society does. Such ethics never asks the two most important questions: What is man? and What is the purpose of his life on this earth?

C. S. Lewis uses the image of the fleet of sailing ships to show that ethics deals with three great questions, not just one. First the ships need to know how to avoid collisions. That is social ethics, and that *is* taught. In the second place, they need to know how to stay shipshape, how to avoid sinking. That is the question of virtues and vices, and that is *not* taught. Finally, they need to know their mission, why they are at sea in the first place. That is the question of the ultimate purpose of human life. It is a religious question, and of course it is not asked, much less answered.

An ethic without bite will offend no one. The one thing no teacher dares to do is to tell anyone he or she is wrong and needs to change. We dare not confront. There is not a single biblical prophet who would be allowed to teach in a modern public university or to talk on network TV today without being labeled "fanatic," "authoritarian," "reactionary," "simplistic," and probably "fundamentalist" (which combines all these horrible things). Jesus Himself—the real Jesus described in the Gospels rather than the meek and gentle Jesus of the selective modern imagination, which is only a thin slice of Him—would be the most radically unacceptable of all. He would be crucified a second time, in words.

Why have we reduced Him to "meek and gentle Jesus"? Because we have reduced all the virtues to one, being nice, and we measure Jesus by our standards instead of measuring our standards by Him.

But why have we reduced all the virtues to being nice? Because we have reduced all the goods to one, the one that kindness ministers to: pleasure, comfort, happiness. We have reduced ourselves to pleasure-seeking animals.

But why have we reduced ourselves to pleasure-seeking animals? Because we are implicit materialists. Our ethics are always rooted in our metaphysics, and modern ethics is rooted in modern metaphysics, the modern world-view, which is the superstition that all that is objectively real is nature (Naturalism).

THE CHRISTIAN RESPONSE TO THE CRISIS

How have Christians responded to modern man's loss of the knowledge of virtue?

Modernist or liberal Christians in all churches and denominations essentially reduce religion to morality. Thus they specialize in morality. Christianity to them is essentially an ethic, a way of living in this world rather than a way of attaining the next. Christ becomes essentially a teacher and example rather than God our Savior. (He is both, of course; liberal Christianity is half-Christianity, not non-Christianity.) Ethics then becomes supremely important for the modernist. It's his "thing," all he has left. The principle is obvious: The specialty shop does good work. Preaching, for instance, is supremely important for Protestants, and Protestants usually do a much better job of preaching than do the Catholics or Orthodox. Similarly, modernists usually do a better job at social ethics than do evangelical Christians.

Yet even here, perhaps, they do not. Let us reconsider our principle of "specialty shops." To isolate a part of a living whole is not only to miss out on the other parts but also to pervert the isolated part. Idolize any part of life, sex, money, drink, a hobby, and sooner or later you will lose the real enjoyment of it as well as of the rest. It becomes an addiction. So the modernist, idolizing social action, often perverts it by collectivizing, organizing, and establishing it to death. He is usually more or less socialistic; and socialists miss not only the greatness of the individual but also the greatness of society, for a natural and happy association of free and generous individuals is more of a society than a mass of organized, bureaucratic, and socialized charities.

By overemphasizing society and underemphasizing individuals, socialism does injustice not only to individuals but also to society. Likewise, by overemphasizing ethics and underemphasizing religion, modernism does injustice not only to religion but also to ethics. How does that work? Ethics without religion means sin without salvation. Though modernists avoid both these religious terms, their concentration on ethics really fosters the very thing modernism accuses its enemy, fundamentalism, of fostering:

guilt. That's why the modernist is always busily do-gooding. He has the same problem Martin Luther had before he discovered the gospel. And the problem of guilt is even greater for the modernist than for the fundamentalist, for even if the fundamentalist over-emphasizes sin, he at least offers hope of salvation.

What has been the orthodox Christians' response to the modern values-vacuum?

Conservative Protestants, both evangelicals and fundamentalists, have not been able to fill the ethical needs of our time mainly because of their suspicion of a traditional natural law ethic of virtues and vices with a foundation in a rational knowledge of human nature. They are suspicious of this approach as pagan, Greek, Roman Catholic, humanistic, rationalistic, or naturalistic. They think it results in a two-layer cake, with natural virtue on the bottom and supernatural virtue on the top. One of the purposes of this book is to show the oneness of the two; the two parts of this book fit together like body and soul.

One of the most serious faults in the evangelical and fundamentalist ethic is its passivity. Its adherents say, "The Lord will work it out." Yes, and meanwhile the Lord has commanded us to act, not just to wait. The Lord is our heavenly Father, and fathers want their children to grow up and think and act for themselves. To insist that we take responsibility for ourselves and cultivate virtue is not to think that we work our way into heaven by piling up Brownie points with God. It is to see us as human beings rather than as wax impresses, to interpret the image of God properly (God is active and so are we), to see our proper response to God as a full and human one, and to distinguish justification (which is God's alone) from sanctification (which is ours *and* God's).

Conservative Protestants also often take an anti-intellectual, anti-rational attitude and are suspicious of traditional ethics for its reliance on human reason. There are two things to be said against this. The first is the theoretical point that reason, though fallen like the rest of us, is still part of God's image in us and is to be used, not despised. The second is the practical, tactical point that we can win battles using reason.

To explain this second point, consider the problem of communicating with a non-Christian world if you abandon an ethic based at least partly on natural human reason. If we preach our ethics only from Scripture and faith and ignore God-given reason, then we have no common starting point and no common ground for dialogue with unbelievers on crucial issues like abortion and nuclear war. The case against abortion can be made on a purely rational basis, a basis the opponents will have to listen to, a basis they cannot fault as biased, a basis that will reveal their own position to be irrational. When we can clobber them with their own weapons, we are silly to retreat into our own weapon house, which they declare out of bounds. When we can beat them at their own game, we are silly to insist on playing ours when they will not. (If anyone doubts that the case against abortion can be made definitively on purely rational grounds, I offer my own modest effort, *The Unaborted Socrates*.)

On the Roman Catholic side, some writers continue to write and argue on the basis of a traditional natural law and natural reason ethic with its scheme of vices and virtues; but some Catholic thinkers ignore this tradition and label it "pre-Vatican II," as if Vatican II instituted a new ethic and a new religion. Many Catholic theologians, like their Protestant counterparts, have sold out to modernism. But the magisterium (the official teaching authority of the Church) has not, nor has the current philosopher-king, a personalist-phenomenologist philosopher named John Paul II.

Although this approach was common to main-line Christianity for nearly two millennia, both modernists and fundamentalists have abandoned rational ethics based on human nature, with natural as well as supernatural virtues and vices. Modernists and fundamentalists now are really in agreement about the impotence of reason and the unknowability of human nature as it really is.

Evangelicals are poised between these two options. Historically suspicious of the traditional Catholic approach, they are rethinking this opposition, as Catholics are rethinking their anti-Protestant prejudices. A new alignment is being forged. Catholics are rediscovering the need for evangelism and evangelicals are rediscovering the need for liturgy, sacrament, and church unity. The crucial issue of our day that is forging this new alliance more than any religious issue is the issue of abortion.

Since evangelicals, like Catholics, usually believe in objective morality, they want to avoid the silliness of saying, "I'm personally opposed to abortion, but I wouldn't dream of imposing my morality on others." There are only two places to look for the origin of this morality, God and human nature. Catholics, on paper at least, look to both. God is the ultimate origin, and human nature made in His image is the proximate origin of morality. Natural law morality means both a morality known to natural reason and a morality based on human nature.

But a secular society will not look to God. Therefore if we will not look to human nature, we have no meeting place. Why should Christians be afraid to look to human nature? It is fallen and defaced, yes, but a marred painting is still a painting. A sick man is still a man, with human needs. Both natural and even supernatural virtues are based on human needs, which are based on human nature in itself, in its relation to other human beings, and in its relation to God. A full ethic has all three dimensions, like C. S. Lewis's fleet of sailing ships.

Let us sketch such an ethic.

CHAPTER TWO

Western Culture on the Couch:
A Spiritual Psychoanalysis

When a patient is sick, a medical analysis is in order, and nearly all thoughtful observers agree that Western civilization is sick. We need, therefore, a medical analysis of Western civilization.

I mean by a medical analysis not an analysis of our material illnesses, such as poverty or starvation, but of our spiritual illnesses. It would be an analysis of the soul, not of the body; of the psyche, not of the soma. It would be a cultural psychoanalysis, for civilizations, like individuals, have souls; and souls, like bodies, have diseases. Many individuals are hurting inside and going to soul doctors, psychologists and psychiatrists, because our civilization is hurting inside.

A medical analysis can apply to the soul as well as to the body because a human being is a psychosomatic unity; there is always a connection between the two. Material starvation, for example, is a symptom of a spiritual starvation; an external war is the externalization of an internal war.

Anyone whose common sense has not been dulled by familiarity should be able to see the blindingly obvious truth that there is something radically wrong with a civilization in which millions devote their lives to pointless luxuries that do not even make them happy, while millions of others are starving, a civilization where no hand, voluntary or involuntary, moves money from luxury yachts to starving babies fast enough to save the babies. It does not take a moralist to see that there is something not working in a civilization where, as C. S. Lewis says, "their rapid production of food leaves half of them starving, their aphrodisiacs make them impotent, and their labor-saving devices have banished leisure from their land."

THE FOUR STEPS OF A MEDICAL ANALYSIS

All practical philosophers, that is, all seekers of wisdom who think about what to do and how to live, say four basic things about us, simply because the structure of our existence is such that there *are* only four basic things to say, four basic questions to answer. These are the four steps of a *medical* analysis:

1. *Observation* of symptoms
2. *Diagnosis* of disease
3. *Prognosis* of cure
4. *Prescription* for treatment

The symptoms are the undesired effects, and disease is the undesired cause; the cure is the desired effect, and the treatment is the desired cause. When we combine the objective scientific law of cause and effect with the subjective human desire to avoid suffering and evil and to attain happiness and good, we get to the four steps of any practical analysis:

1. The problem (undesired effect)
2. The cause of the problem (the undesired cause)
3. The solution (the desired effect)
4. The cause of the solution (the desired cause)

Let us look at several proposed solutions to our vacuum of virtue based on this simple analysis grid.

PLATO'S FOUR NOBLE TRUTHS

Plato said nearly everything there was to say in philosophy. Ralph Waldo Emerson said, "Plato is philosophy and philosophy is Plato." Alfred North Whitehead described the whole history of Western philosophy as a series of "footnotes to Plato." Yet the practical teaching of the father of philosophy is startlingly simple and can be summarized in four points. Whether it is true or not is another question, a question I would not answer simply yes or simply no; but I only want to show the *structure* of his thought here.

1. Our problem, most generally, is that we are not good. We are full of vices.
2. The cause of this is ignorance. We do evil because we ignorantly think it will be good for us. The thief fails to obey the advice of the oracle, "Know thyself," because he thinks he is a body, or even a wallet, rather than a soul. That is the reason why he ignorantly thinks stolen money will do him more good than virtue.
3. The solution to the world's problems is virtue. Good individuals make a good society, as Plato outlines in *The Republic*.
4. The way to virtue is knowledge of the Good. If we knew without a doubt that virtue was always for our good, that "justice is always more profitable than injustice" (the central teaching of *The Republic*), then we would have no motive for preferring vice. We must therefore teach virtue, both individually, as Socrates did by his famous Socratic method, and socially, by an ideal educational system in an ideal state.

THE STOICS' FOUR NOBLE TRUTHS

The teachings of the Stoics, those ancient Greeks whose philosophy is experiencing a remarkable comeback in contemporary pop psychology, can be capsuled along the same four lines.

1. We are unhappy, anxious, and full of suffering
2. because of our passions
3. but we can attain peace of mind
4. by cultivating *apatheia*, "passionlessness" (in modern terms, "be cool").

Stoicism is essentially a nonmystical and nonreligious form of Buddhism. The essence of Buddhism is nothing but Buddha's so-called "Four Noble Truths":

1. that all of life is suffering, or out-of-jointness (*dukkha*);
2. that the cause is greed, or selfish desire (*tanha*);
3. that the way to the "extinction" (*nirvana*) of suffering is the extinction of selfish desire;
4. and that the way to the extinction of selfish desire is the Buddhist yoga of "the noble eightfold path" of purification and ego-reduction.

CHRIST'S FOUR NOBLE TRUTHS

Can Christ's teachings be summarized in these four steps too? They certainly can. And it would be a great advantage for Christians to see this, an advantage both for themselves, so that they do not lose sight of the forest for the trees, and for apologetic purposes, to show to the world simply and clearly what, essentially, Christianity is.

1. The most spectacular symptom of our spiritual disease is *death*. Christ came to conquer death. He is the only man in history who did.
2. The cause of death is *sin*. Adam (the word also means "mankind") chose sin, separation from God, from God's will, from God's fellowship. This separation entered into our very

being, for our being is dependent on our relationship with God, the Creator of our very being. Sin is the separation of the soul from God; death is the separation of the body from the soul.

3. We can't save ourselves from sin, no matter what we do. The leopard can't change his spots. However God saves us from sin by sending His Son to earth to become a man, to live a sinless life, to die, to rise from the dead, and to take glorified human nature to Heaven. The cure has many different names. Some of them are: "salvation," "regeneration," "justification," "eternal life," "sanctifying grace," "the kingdom of God," and "the kingdom of Heaven."

4. The prescription for salvation is *faith*. *Believing* in Christ is the cause of *receiving* Christ, being incorporated into Christ or, as Christ Himself put it, being "born again."

Death, sin, salvation, faith—it's all here. Putting the Christian message into just four points helps us notice something in the big picture that we may have overlooked. We may have missed the fact that Christ came to solve two related problems, sin and death, and that physical life and death are connected casually with spiritual life (salvation) and death (sin). It shows also that the two opposite options are estrangement and union, sin and faith, a fundamental no to God and a fundamental yes. The opposite of sin is not virtue but faith (virtue is the fruit of faith) and the opposite of faith is not doubt but sin ("whatever is not from faith is sin," says Saint Paul).

Christian thinkers throughout history have emphasized different aspects of Christianity that also fit the fourfold structure. For instance, (1) Martin Luther's problem was a nagging guilt that no amount of good works could relieve. (2) He perceived that it was his attempt to justify himself that exacerbated rather than removed his guilt and that (3) he was already justified, deguiltified with God by (4) faith in Christ.

In *Pensées*, Blaise Pascal, the first deep observer of the modern spirit, observed a new phenomenon in modern man, one so new that there was a new word for it, *ennui,* "boredom." (1) He observed the new, sophisticated, jaded modern person to be bored and fleeing boredom by a thousand diversions or by indifference to his eternal destiny. (2) He saw that this boredom and flight from self came from a state of wretchedness. It's no fun to face and admit one's inner emptiness, so we reserve as the supreme punishment for our most desperate criminals the very thing the ancient sages longed for as a supreme gift, solitude. (3) However, eternal happiness with God and the hope for it in time are available even to skeptical modernity which lacks both of the two traditional ways to God, faith and reason, (4) through a "wager." It is a foolish bet not to believe in God because if there is no God, there are no eternal rewards or punishments, so there is nothing to be gained or lost. However if there is a God, the only chance of winning is to bet on Him and the only chance of losing is to bet against Him.

Sören Kierkegaard, a little later, observed (1) a deep underlying despair in the very brilliance and success of the modern man of the world. (2) He diagnosed it as due to the fundamental categories under which he lived, which he called "the aesthetic way of life." This sees nothing more than pleasures and pains, interests and boredoms. (3) Full, authentic human existence can be attained when the emptiness of the aesthetic life ("vanity of vanities") and its despair are exchanged for an ethical and then a religious existence. (4) This can be done only by a leap into a fundamentally different set of categories, another dimension. In the ethical category, good and evil replace pleasure and pain as ultimates, and in the religious category, we find dawning on our horizon a relationship with God and with it the new categories of sin (the no-relationship) and faith (the yes-relationship).

SECULARISTS' FOUR NOBLE TRUTHS

René Descartes, the father of modern philosophy, is of a more theoretical, less practical bent; yet even in him we see our fourfold structure. (1) Uncertainty in philosophy results from (2) unscientific methods. (3) Certainty can result from (4) a new method, essentially the scientific method applied to philosophy, which he proposed in his *Discourse on Method*. In turn, this theoretical certainty would have momentous practical application: the conquest of ignorance, prejudice, and therefore war, and the technological conquest of nature, including perhaps disease and death itself.

Karl Marx has changed modern history more than any other thinker. His philosophy too can be summarized in four simple points. (1) Alienation of worker from his work and of class from class is due to (2) the capitalist system of the bourgeoisie's exploitation of the proletariat (the haves against the have-nots). (3) However a classless society of peace, plenty, and prosperity for all ("from each according to his abilities, to each according to his needs") will result from (4) a communist revolution in which the bourgeoisie are eliminated. All the complexity and millions of pages of Marxist philosophy come down to this simple and therefore attractive bottom line.

Freud's psychology also fits our fourfold structure. (1) Neurosis and psychosis are caused by (2) the maladjustment or conflict between the id and the superego (animal drives and social conscience), which in turn has other causes such as the need for repression inherent in civilization itself. (3) However a reasonable adjustment, compromise, balance, or homeostasis can result from (4) psychoanalysis, in which the mere fact of becoming aware of inner conflicts and their causes can liberate one from their power.

THE FOUR NOBLE TRUTHS

	SYMPTOMS	DIAGNOSIS	PROGNOSIS	PRESCRIPTION
Buddha	suffering	desire	nirvana	ego-reduction
Stoicism	anxiety	passion	peace	passionlessness
Plato	vice	ignorance	virtue	knowledge
Christ	death	sin	salvation	faith
Luther	guilt	self-justification	justification	faith
Pascal	boredom	wretchedness	hope	the "wager"
Kierkegaard	despair	aesthetic existence	authentic existence	ethical and religious "leap"
Descartes	uncertainty	unscientific methods	certainty	scientific method
Marx	alienation	capitalism	classless society	communist revolution
Freud	neurosis & psychosis	maladjustment	adjustment	psychoanalysis

FIGURE 2

A person can progress from the unhappiness that cannot be handled to unhappiness that can be handled, which is all Freud ever promised.

The point has been shown in sufficient detail. A four-step analysis of the human spiritual condition is in the tradition of the great sages, the practical philosophers. If we are at all interested in their question of how to live (and if we are not, we are less than fully human, less than fully honest), then we too must ask these four questions. They are inherent in the very structure of our existence.

Let us therefore continue our analysis of the spiritual disease of our civilization. We have seen the symptoms (the First Noble Truth) in chapter one. We have justified a four-step medical analysis here in chapter two. We must now examine the historical causes of our disease (the Second Noble Truth) in chapter three, and then propose a prescription for a cure in the rest of the book.

CHAPTER THREE

*Spiritual History 101:
How Did We Get to the Edge?*

The story of our civilization can be told from different viewpoints.
The history books tell it from only one point of view, and not the
most important one at that. What makes headlines to the historian
is not necessarily what makes headlines to God, Who reads hearts
while we read appearances.

Furthermore God knows the meaning of history better than the
historians do, because history is "His story." He is its Author and
we are its characters. It is true that human free choices move history, but so does God; just as Captain Ahab moves the plot of *Moby
Dick,* but so does Melville.

We cannot fully possess God's point of view, of course, but we
can seek it and approach it, rather than ignore it. We can also pay
attention when God reveals some clues to it. So let's try to write a
short summary of the spiritual history of Western civilization, a
history not of its body but of its soul.

Its overall structure will look like a lazy *H*:

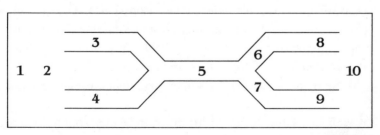

FIGURE 3

Think of two rivers emerging from a swamp, joining, parting again, and reentering the swamp. The steps along the way in this story are the ten key periods of our spiritual history:

1. The period of myth
2. The dawn of self-consciousness, the axial period
3. Hebraism: virtue in practice
4. Hellenism: virtue in theory
5. The medieval Christian synthesis
6. The Renaissance: the return to Hellenism
7. The Reformation: the return to Hebraism
8. Classical modernity: Enlightenment rationalism, Hellenism secularized
9. Antimodernity: Romantic irrationalism, Hebraism secularized
10. The postmodern period, the present: a new axial period?

1. *Myth*. For well over 90 percent of the time that our species has lived on this planet, we have thought and lived by myth. Yet we know and care less about this long and formative period of time than about any other, probably because of our chronological snobbery.

The word *myth* means "story." Myths are moving pictures that arise from the imagination, that great, creative, unconscious well of wisdom within us that psychologists are just beginning to explore in this century. These stories and images that bubble up in myths still move us profoundly on the unconscious level, especially in art, namely, in the cinema, that great waking dream-machine. Jungian psychologists could have a field day with MTV videos; they are chock-full of archetypes, mythic images.

Myth is immediate and spontaneous. It has beauty but not truth, except the truth of beauty itself. It may sound profound to say with Keats that "beauty is truth, truth beauty," but it is really

THE THREE PROPHETS IN THE HUMAN SOUL

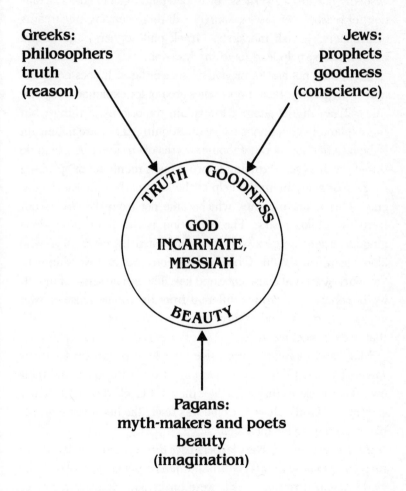

Greeks:
philosophers
truth
(reason)

Jews:
prophets
goodness
(conscience)

TRUTH GOODNESS

GOD
INCARNATE,
MESSIAH

BEAUTY

Pagans:
myth-makers and poets
beauty
(imagination)

Figure 4

confusion. I mean no disrespect for beauty, which is one of God's three great prophets in the human soul, the other two being goodness and truth. Beauty is known by the imagination; goodness, by conscience; and truth, by reason (in the large, ancient sense of wisdom, not just cleverness; of understanding, not just calculation; of reason, not just reason*ing*). All three converging streams of prophets, Jewish moralists, Greek philosophers, and pagan myth-makers, help lead us to the Messiah.

Myth does not ask for or give reasons or laws. It does not question or command. Its initiation rites are not for explanation or morality. True, myths attempt to explain the origins of things, but this explanation does not survive questioning. They are not meant to be rational nor moral, although myths often direct people to do things, such as self-torturing to prove one's manhood or speaking magic words to obtain the help of the local gods to defeat the enemy. This is not morality, which came not from the priests but from the philosophers. The exception is the Jews, who alone among ancient peoples were not dominated by myth, and who alone identified the one Object of religious awe and worship with the source of moral conscience and law. The innate sense of morality, or conscience, is quite different from the innate sense of awe, wonder, worship, and transcendent mystery ("the numinous") that is expressed by myth.

Myth and morality existed side by side in paganism for thousands of years. Only one people joined them together, and their own records claim that it was not they but God who did it. Their claim to be God's chosen people was really the humblest of possible explanations for their genius.

2. *The axial period.* Karl Jaspers uses this term for the sixth century B.C. because in this century human consciousness all over the world began turning, as if it were on its axis, and facing itself. Consciousness became self-conscious, or reflective. This hap-

pened independently at approximately the same time all over the world. It was either a coincidence or a plot, either chance or divine providence. The more we look, the less it looks like chance.

In China, for instance, we find the two great figures of Confucius and Lao-Tzu. Confucius substituted deliberate tradition for "traditional tradition," and Lao-Tzu substituted the individual mystical experience of the Tao, or cosmic life-force, for the authoritarian and impersonal fortunetelling of the *I Ching,* in his little masterpiece, the *Tao Te Ching.*

In India, Gautama the Buddha abandoned the books and authority of the Brahmins to seek Nirvana deliberately and told the world that anyone could do the same: "Be ye lamps unto yourselves."

In Persia, Zoroaster substituted prophetic and moralistic religion for animism, tribalism, and nature-worship.

In Greece, philosophers and scientists began the revolutionary act of asking questions of the world and life, questions that the poets and myth-makers could not answer.

In Israel, the great prophets demanded personal and social justice and holiness, not just ritual observance.

Everywhere, in different ways, human consciousness was making new, inward demands, becoming aware of its own powers and responsibilities. In a sense modern man was born twenty-six centuries ago. Each of the subsequent events in our spiritual history is dependent on this event, in this new context.

3. *Hellenism* is Matthew Arnold's name for the Greek spirit. Even when political Hellas (Greece) died, its spirit was preserved in a Roman body, so that we can meaningfully use the single term "classical" for both Greek and Roman culture.

The Greeks, to put it very simply, thought and talked more than anyone else. Luke, writing Acts, has to explain to his non-Greek audience this strange Greek behavior: "All the Athenians and the foreigners who were there spent their time in nothing else but either to tell or to hear some new thing" (17:21). The most important word in their language was *logos,* which meant (among other things) "word, language, discourse, thought, reason, or intelligible truth." Thus John begins his gospel with the astonishing claim that the *logos* which the Greeks searched for, the Truth, existed as God and with God "in the beginning" and "became flesh" as Jesus, the Jesus who said, "I AM the Truth."

The kind of truth these thinking, talking, and searching Greeks thought, talked, and searched the most about was the truth about *virtue.* Socrates, the greatest of them, one of the two or three men in the history of this planet who made the greatest difference and the greatest contribution to all subsequent ages, thought about almost nothing else. Each of his dialogues is a quest for the truth about some particular virtue.

We can contrast the Hellenic and the Hebraic minds as Matthew Arnold does, by contrasting theory with practice, intellectualism with voluntarism, the centrality of thought with the centrality of will, choice, and action. The Greeks represented virtue in theory, thinking about virtue; the Hebrews represented virtue in practice. For Socrates and Plato, right thinking *is* virtue. Virtue is knowledge and knowledge is virtue. If we only know what is good, we will do it. The will, choice, and action necessarily follow thinking. We always choose what we think is profitable to us. If our thoughts are right, our choices will be right. Thus philosophical wisdom is the prescription for a moral utopia, as Plato set out in his *Republic.*

4. *Hebraism.* Two crucial categories of human existence were missing from the Greek scheme, if we take the Hebrew and Christian perspective: sin and faith, the categories of relationship with God. They are religious categories, not just ethical ones. The religious includes the ethical but goes beyond it. The religious Jew and Christian are to be ethically virtuous, of course, but also reli-

giously faithful. Of the two great commandments, the first is religious (to love the Lord with the whole heart), the second is ethical (to love neighbor as self).

For Hebraism, faith (fidelity) is first; virtue, second; and knowledge, third in importance. The *knowledge* of God and virtue is not prior to the practice of them, as it was for the Greeks. Rather, it is embedded in or dependent on the practice. Thus Jesus gives the perfectly Hebraic answer to the question: "How can we know your teaching, whether it is from God or not?" when He says: "If your will were to do the will of my Father, you would know my teaching, that it comes from Him." For the Greek, head judges heart: "Live according to reason." For the Jew, heart judges head: "Keep thy heart with all diligence, for out of it are the issues of life." (*Heart* in the Bible means "will," not "sentiment." Hebraism is practical, not sentimental.)

5. *The medieval Christian synthesis.* Christian virtue is not fundamentally different from Hebrew virtue, because not only Jews and Christians but nearly everyone knows what is right and wrong (religions do not differ much in their ethics, but in their theology) and because Jews and Christians believe in the same God, the author of the moral law.

But Christianity, unlike Judaism, is a proselytizing religion. It sent missionaries out into the Greco-Roman world to convert it, and the "it" to be converted included Greek notions of virtue.

There were from the beginning three different attitudes on the part of Christians to the pagan world in general and to pagan notions of virtue in particular: (1) uncritical synthesis, (2) critical synthesis, and (3) criticism and antisynthesis. Christians accepted either (1) all, (2) some, or (3) none of the Greek ideals of virtue. The greatest and mainstream Christians, like Augustine and Aquinas, took the second way and have been criticized by extremists of both wings right up to the present day, labeled fundamentalists by the modernists and modernists by the fundamentalists.

Perhaps *synthesis* is the wrong word for the great tradition forged in the thousand and more years of the Middle Ages. It was rather a profound Christian reinterpretation of Greek philosophy and Greek morality. It was not like gluing a rabbit onto a carrot but like a rabbit's eating and digesting a carrot.

6 and 7. *The Renaissance and the Reformation.* Two forces separated the strands of the rope that the Middle Ages tied together. We no longer live in the Middle Ages, mainly because of the Renaissance and the Reformation.

The Renaissance tried to return to the Greco-Roman classicism and humanism minus the medieval additions of scholastic philosophy and theology. The Reformation tried to return to a simpler, premedieval, New Testament Christianity, a Christianity minus the additions of Greek rationalism and Roman legalism and institutionalism which the reformers thought had corrupted the Catholic Church. From our vantage point today we call the Renaissance and the Reformation progressive movements because they led out of the Middle Ages into the modern world. However, thinkers in those times saw themselves as part of nostalgic or returning movements, purifying movements: the Renaissance returning to Hellenism, the Reformation to Hebraism.

The dichotomy is still with us. Hebraism and Hellenism, heart and head, will and reason, are still separated. Nietzsche's unsuccessful attempt to find the unifying center of these two forces (which he called the "Dionysian" and the "Apollonian" after the Greek gods of earth and sky, darkness and light, vegetation and the sun) drove him insane. Along the road to madness, brilliance was thrown off, like sparks from a destructive fire. All this is true for our whole civilization as well as for Nietzsche. I am not glorifying a madman, but Nietzsche was a prophet and a mirror to the madness of our own civilization, and we can learn much from him.

8. *The Enlightenment*. The term is ironic; for spiritually the eighteenth century was the darkest ever. Scientism and rationalism replaced faith; the human heart narrowed and hardened in conformity with its own gods, the inventions of its own hands. G. K. Chesterton was profoundly right about the three eras of our history, ancient, medieval, and modern (pre-Christian, Christian, and post-Christian) when he said that "paganism was the biggest thing in the world, and Christianity was bigger, and everything since has been comparatively small."

Enlightenment rationalism cut off the top of Greek ideals and kept the bottom; cut off wisdom and kept logic, transformed reason into reasoning. With this new, streamlined tool, the world could be conquered. The scientific method became the tool for the new goal, "man's conquest of nature." Alexander Pope summarized the faith of the Enlightenment in two lines:

> Nature and Nature's laws lay hid in night;
> God said, "Let Newton be!" and all was light.

9. *Romanticism*. Nineteenth-century Romanticism and its philosophical child, Existentialism, was the reaction against Enlightenment rationalism, the reaction of heart against head. But just as the Enlightenment's head was a trimmed-down and secularized head, Romanticism's heart was a trimmed-down and secularized heart, exhibiting sentiment instead of will, in relationship to nature rather than to God.

10. *The present*. Where do we go from here? Nearly everyone agrees that we are standing at the end of an age, perhaps at a new axial period. We have left modernity behind almost as surely as we have left antiquity behind. We are postmodern. But we do not yet know what that means.

From our unique experiment in living without a set of objective values, only two roads lie open, return or destruction. Once the sled is on the slippery slope leading to the abyss, we either brake or break; and no amount of rhetoric about progress can alter that fact. Crying "progress" as we die will not raise us from death.

Yet our diagnosis gives us reason to hope. We came from a place closer to home; therefore it is possible to return. Our illness is not wholly hereditary. There is, of course, a far deeper illness in us that *is* hereditary. It is called "Original Sin," and for that a remedy far deeper than philosophy is needed, and in fact has been provided, and that is "the greatest story ever told."

But there is also a cure, a hope, a home to return to on the natural level. It is our own human nature. The four cardinal virtues, which we shall explore in chapter four, are the heart of natural morality, and they lie embedded and ineradicable in our very nature. That nature is weakened and perverted by sin, but it is not obliterated. Natural virtue cannot save our souls, but it can save our civilization, and that is no mean feat. But it can save us only if we both know it and practice it.

On the supernatural level there is also hope because there too is a home from which we came, Paradise, though the road back is only by grace. Since we were once home, there *is* home and thus a hope, a possibility of return, or even something better. The road to Paradise is supernatural virtue, the three theological virtues of faith, hope, and charity and the blessedness, or beatitude, that flows from them.

PART II

The Key: Personal Virtue

CHAPTER FOUR

Justice, Wisdom, Courage, and Moderation: The Four Cardinal Virtues

The four cardinal virtues—*justice, wisdom* (prudence), *courage* (fortitude), and *moderation* (self-control, temperance)—come not just from Plato or Greek philosophy. You will find them in Holy Scripture. They are knowable by human nature, which God designed. Plato first formulated them, but he did for virtue only what Newton did for motion: He discovered and tabulated its own inherent foundational laws.

These four are called "cardinal" virtues from _carde,_ which is Latin for "hinge." All other virtues hinge on these four. That includes lesser virtues, which are corollaries of these, and also greater virtues, which are the flower of these.

These four cardinal virtues are not the only virtues, or even the highest ones. As Einstein surpassed Newton, Jesus most certainly surpassed Plato. But just as Einstein did not contradict Newton but included him, presupposed him, and built on him, so Jesus' supernatural virtues do not contradict Plato's natural virtues but presuppose them. Plato gives us virtue's grammar; Jesus gives us virtue's poetry.

BACK TO THE FUTURE!

During the Silly Sixties, I was teaching a course in ethics at Boston College to a class of idealistic, impatient, and antihistorical freshmen whose vision of history was the Dark Ages and then Us. They were eager to save the world, design a new society, and liberate themselves and everyone else, especially those who did not want to be liberated, from the terrible, tyrannical past and to create a "brave new world" for the bright future. So my assigned reading list composed of Plato, Aristotle, Augustine, and Aquinas hardly turned them on. "We know so much more than the past did," they said, and they were not impressed with my comeback from T. S. Eliot: "Yes, and they are that which we know."

So they asked me whether we could do something more "relevant," something more experimental, something like what other classes were doing: designing their own course instead of being "enslaved" to the hoary past and to the "imposed values" of the teacher. I decided to go along with their scheme for a trial run. I said I'd play Socrates with them and together we'd try to design a new ethic for a new society, from scratch. I would only be their Socratic questioner, not their lecturer.

They were thrilled.

Off and running we went, throwing our books temporarily into the ragbag or dustbin of history and consulting only our precious creativity. Now what values do we want in this new society? First of all, do we want a double standard? A different ethic for society and for individuals? No, that was the hypocrisy of past and present establishments. No double standard.

All right, next, what does society need? Harmony, cooperation, togetherness, working as one, each doing the thing he or she can do best for others, for the community, doing your own thing and communalism at once. That sounds like a very progressive notion of justice, better than the old legalistic one. In fact, it sounds like music, which they loved very much. True justice is social music, harmony. What an enlightened idea!

What next? What qualities must the leaders have? Not wealth, not power, not privilege, not even sheer intelligence or cleverness, but understanding, insight, sympathy. Into what? Human nature, human needs, human values. And this understanding of theirs has to have a practical side to it. The leaders should know people and their problems and be able to solve them, not just know some abstract ideal. What a nice, relevant redefinition of wisdom!

What about heroism? Do we value that, in society and in individuals? Oh, yes. The willingness to freely go beyond the call of duty, to make sacrifices, to choose the difficult thing, to take chances. Courage. Not just folly, recklessness, not just physical strength, not even just physical courage, the ability to endure pain, but moral courage, the willingness to act on your convictions even if it costs you something, such as convenience or social acceptance. What a great new notion of courage! How unbarbarian! How deep! How superior to tradition! We must *know* when to fight and when to flee, what to fear and what not to fear.

Now what about greed? Is that a virtue? No. Capitalism is wicked because it fosters greed, materialism, consumerism. But are material things evil in themselves? Oh, no. We should be sensitive to material pleasures, but small is beautiful. We should desire and get and use just what we naturally and truly need, not what the admen tell us and sell us. If we all practiced Thoreau's or Buddha's detachment from greed, our present economy would soon collapse. Well then, let it.

Let us make a new one, where only natural needs are satisfied. A noneconomistic economy, where people make and use what they truly need. Material things are our servants, not our masters; our horses, not our riders. We shouldn't let them ride us, neither should we lock them up in the stable; but we should "ride the wild horses," our own desires and the pleasures we take in material things. It's a good world, but we should treat it as a work of art, raw material for beauty, not conquest. What an enlightened new alternative to both materialism *and* Puritanism! (They knew nothing about the real Puritans, of course.)

And these new values fit the new psychology. Freud showed us what we are, id, ego, and superego; and moderation is the value for the id, for animal desires; courage is the value for the ego, or will; and wisdom is the value for the superego, or conscience, or mind. Our new values fit our nature. Justice is the harmony or integration or adjustment (what nice modern-sounding words!) of all the different parts. A really up-to-date picture!

Now someone who lived like this—wouldn't he or she be happy? Yes. Happiness, that's the great thing, the daring new answer to the question: "What's it all about, Alfie?" Let's free ourselves from legalism, moralism, and guilt, to pursue our own happiness. An individual who lived according to these values would be truly and naturally happy, even if not rich and powerful. Happiness comes from within, not from without; that's the great new secret we have discovered. The sons have become wiser than the fathers. We have found life's great secret for ourselves.

And the same would be true for society. Any society patterned on these principles would be happy, just as individuals would. No double standard, remember. We have here a bold new prescription for human happiness. Our new notion of justice is the true profit. Not money but natural justice is true profit. This justice is always more profitable than anything else, any alternative to justice, any injustice. Justice is more profitable than injustice.

Perhaps we should write all this up, put down our new discoveries in a book for the world, a new book for a new age. How exciting!

Unless—unless it may have been done before? How would you know whether it has or not? You've scorned the past. Are you quite sure what it is you've scorned? Let's just take one sample drilling from the soil of the past. Let's look at the first and oldest philosophical ethic and politic in our civilization, Plato's *The Republic*. Let's test old Plato by our new wisdom and see how he scores. Might he have anticipated any of our ideas?

The reader who has read *The Republic* can anticipate the next step. The students were truly amazed to find that all eight of the ideas they had just discovered were precisely the main points of this bewhiskered old classic: no double standard; justice as harmony; wisdom as understanding; courage as nonphysical; moderation versus materialism; the fit between the three virtues and the three parts of the soul; the fact that justice leads to happiness for individuals and societies, that "justice is more profitable than injustice"; and overall the use of rational discovery and persuasion rather than force.

After reading all this in *The Republic* they wanted to read more "old stuff." So we read Plato's *Gorgias*, Aristotle's *Nicomachean Ethics*, Augustine's *Confessions*, and even parts of Aquinas's *Summa Theologiae*. They found Aquinas's treatise on happiness (*Summa* I-II, question 2, "On Those Things in Which Happiness Consists") a particularly "relevant" reading, for they could classify all their friends and all their favorite characters in fiction as pursuing one or another of the candidates for happiness that Aquinas listed, explored—and refuted.

A HEALTHY SOUL

Why are these old philosophers so up-to-date? Because they took their bearings not from the date—nothing is so surely and quickly dated as the up-to-date—but from the unchanging essence of man, the inherent structure of the soul. Plato was the first to discover and map this, the first to give us a psychograph. The four cardinal virtues—justice, wisdom, courage, and moderation—are relevant to man in every age because they are relevant to man himself, not to the age. They fit our nature and our nature's needs.

The human body has a situation that is inherent, not socially changeable, and the laws of its health are equally inherent and unchangeable, objective. The same is true of the soul. *Virtue is simply health of soul*. Justice, the overall virtue, is the harmony of the soul, as health is the harmony of the body. Justice is not just paying your debts, not just an external relationship between two or more people, but also and first of all the internal relationship within each individual among the parts of the soul.

The harmony is hierarchical, not egalitarian. When World follows Man, when within Man Body follows Soul, when within Soul Appetites follow Will and Will follows Reason (Wisdom), we have Justice. When the hierarchy is inverted, we have injustice. Will leading Reason is rationalization and propaganda; Appetites leading Will is greed; Body leading Soul is animalism; World leading Man is unfreedom.

Justice is individual before it is social. Robinson Crusoe alone on his desert island before Friday shows up can still be just or unjust. We are just or unjust to ourselves before we are just or unjust to others. Justice is rightness, righteousness. Justice is beauty of soul, soul-art, soul-music.

But does the soul have a structure like the body? Isn't it simply consciousness, like light, with no inherent shape or color or size, receiving all its structure and form from its objects? The things light illuminates have determinate structures, but light itself does not (at least, not that sort of structure—e.g., light has no color). Isn't the soul like light?

No, it is not. It is like the world; it has a structure. We can talk about it and derive an ethic from it. For instance, we can discover that it has three distinct faculties or abilities or powers. We discover this, as Plato first argued, from the experience of inner conflict; when our desires move us to do one thing, our reason informs us not to do that thing, and something else in us sides with either reason or desire and decides the issue. (Plato had only the most rudimentary notion of this other thing, which is really the will. He seemed to identify it with what the medieval Scholastics called "irascible appetite," or the capacity for righteous anger.) From Plato to Freud, common sense, philosophy, and psychology have found themselves talking about some version of this tripartite-soul idea with virtue as its health. This is natural, like a heavy body falling to its natural place, or a wanderer returning home.

MISUNDERSTANDINGS

Some of the more common misunderstandings about the four cardinal virtues, in general and in particular, are the following:

1. They are relative to Plato, or the Greek mind, or pre-Christian paganism.
2. Asserting their importance and universality implicitly teaches that they are salvational, that you get to Heaven by practicing them. (This is, logically speaking, a very silly confusion, but I have even found evangelicals and fundamentalists thinking this way.)
3. They constitute only one subjective preference among many, like a taste in foods rather than like the principles of anatomy.
4. They rest on an outdated, simplistic psychology (psychology has grown, but on these foundations).
5. Wisdom means only intelligence rather than understanding—the confusion between cleverness and insight, calculation and contemplation.
6. Wisdom is one-sided, starry-eyed, unworldly, and impractical.

7. Wisdom is only a subjective habit of mind rather than an insight into objectively existing things.
8. Courage means only "taking dares," or foolhardiness.
9. Courage is a specialty for soldiers rather than a necessary aspect of every virtue.
10. Courage is a hard, old-fashioned, no-longer-needed virtue (read Alexander Solzhenitsyn's Harvard commencement address on that one).
11. Moderation means suppression or repression.
12. Moderation is cowardly rather than passionate.
13. Moderation is dull (read G. K. Chesterton's *Orthodoxy* and *The Man Who Was Thursday* to refute that cliché).
14. Justice is a mathematical, impersonal, calculating thing rather than a thing like music.
15. Justice is only external and social.
16. Justice is necessary but unattractive, like a medicine or a law.

There are many more misunderstandings, of course, but it would take a whole book and the demolition of the foundations of the modern mind to explore them all.

A COMMON CHRISTIAN MISUNDERSTANDING

One of the misunderstandings, however, is so important for Christians that it needs special emphasis. That is the one, common in many quarters of modern Christendom, that sees these virtues as a sheer gift of God and not also as hard human work, that sees righteousness as automatically coming with the territory, or part of the package deal of accepting Christ as Lord.

But isn't it true that righteousness, a righteousness far surpassing the four cardinal virtues, becomes available to us when we are joined to Christ? It certainly is! And isn't this a supernatural righteousness, a fruit of the Holy Spirit Himself? Absolutely! But supernatural virtue is not subnatural virtue. It does not dispense with natural human foundations and with our responsibility to be active, not passive, in cultivation of virtuous habits.

A man with a violin case under his arm stood in Times Square looking lost. He asked a policeman, "How can I get to Carnegie Hall?" The policeman answered, "Practice, man, practice." There is no other short cut to sanctity either.

God's word says that "faith without works is dead." The works of virtue are the fruit of faith, that is, of a live faith. Being saintly is our response to being saved. We cannot do either without God but He will not do either without us. He respects our freedom. He makes His power and His grace available to us once we are joined to Christ. But if we simply sit back and let that spiritual capital accumulate in our heavenly bank account without making withdrawals and using it, we are exactly like the wicked and slothful servant who hid his master's money rather than investing it, in Jesus' parable of the talents (see Matt. 25:14–30).

The answer to the faith-and-works issue is essentially a simple one, in fact, startlingly simple. It is that *faith works*. The whole complex question of reconciling Paul's words on faith and James' words on works, and of resolving the dispute that sparked the Reformation, the dispute about justification by faith, is answered at its core at a single stroke: The very same "living water" of God's own Spirit, God's own life in our soul, is received by faith and lived out by virtuous works.

The water of the Sea of Galilee comes from the same source as the water of the Dead Sea, the Jordan River. But the Sea of Galilee stays fresh because it has an outlet for the water it receives. The Dead Sea lives up to its name because it does not.

The same thing happens to the "living waters" from God as to the fresh waters of the Jordan. When we bottle them up inside ourselves, they become stagnant. Stagnant faith stinks, like stagnant water. And the world has sensitive nostrils.

OUR FOUNDATION

These four cardinal virtues are not the only virtues, but they are the *cardes*, "the hinges," on which all the other virtues turn. They are the necessary foundation and precondition for all others. If a person is not courageous, for instance, he will not overcome the difficulties inherent in the practice of any virtue. If he is not wise, he will not understand what he is doing, and his virtue will sink to the level of blind animal instinct.

There are many more virtues than these—there is always more—for "there are more things in heaven and earth than are dreamt of in your philosophy." But never less.

This is the foundation. This must be built, or rebuilt, first. Social and educational experiments must be built on this foundation, or on none. If we are to rebuild our civilization, or if we are to build a new one, we need to build on foundations whose posts reach down into our own being, at least. Ultimately, they must be anchored in God; but we are the image of God.

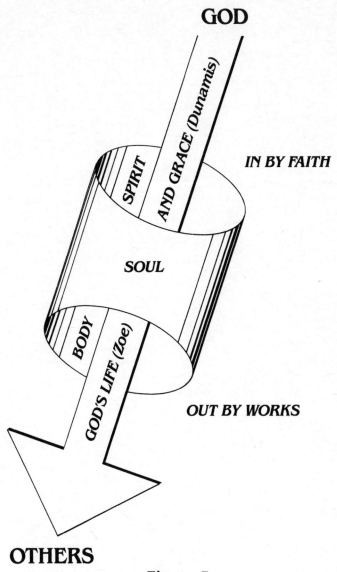

Figure 5

CHAPTER FIVE

Faith, Hope, and Love: The Three Theological Virtues

Evangelicals and fundamentalists often inveigh against the traditional Roman Catholic scheme of the natural and supernatural virtues as a kind of two-layer cake theory. They are reacting against the modernist reductionism of the supernatural to the natural, but they go to the other extreme of denying the independent validity of the natural.

The greatest modern thinker to do the same thing is Kierkegaard (no friend to the fundamentalists, by the way). Kierkegaard makes a very sharp distinction between the ethical (essentially, the natural virtues) and the religious (essentially, the supernatural virtues). Even Saint Augustine called pagan virtues "splendid vices."

Reluctant as I am to disagree with great minds like Kierkegaard and Augustine, I must side with main line Christian orthodoxy here, and with common sense. Of course natural virtues are real virtues, just as natural reason is real reason and natural beauty is real beauty.

True, it does not save you. You do not get to Heaven just by being a little more just, wise, courageous, and temperate. That is not enough. But it *is* good.

It is also a foundation for the supernatural virtues, which *do* get you to Heaven. A person who is unjust, foolish, cowardly, and uncontrolled will find it much harder to believe, to hope in, or to

69

love God. The natural virtues are the seedbed, soil, or fertilizer for the flower of supernatural virtue. Ethics is preparatory to religion, because "the law is our schoolmaster to bring us to Christ."

Having said these good things about natural virtue, it must be added that it is not sufficient, either for the next life or even for this life.

It is not sufficient for the next life even though most non-Christians think it is. If *we* were orchestrating the Last Judgment, we would probably arrange for all the nice people to get to Heaven and none of the nasty people. We are probably puzzled at and perhaps even secretly resentful of God's alternative plan to save only and all those who come to Him in faith, hope, and charity, even if they are failures at the four cardinal virtues. However the reason for God's arrangement is simple: God is love. He wants all of us, even the worst. Only refusal of His gift (grace, forgiveness, Christ) can keep us out of His arms.

Nor are the four cardinal virtues sufficient even for this life. Unless we "seek first the kingdom of God and His righteousness," all these other things will *not* be added to us. Unless we put first things first, second things will not come either. Without the supernatural virtues, the natural virtues fail.

For instance, without charity, which goes beyond justice, no one can be just. We cannot fulfill the requirements of the natural law of justice to our neighbors except by the power of love. "Love is the fulfillment of the law," not by substituting for it, as if we did not need to do the works of justice when we love, but rather by fulfilling it, for when we love someone we want them to receive justice.

Another example is that it is very hard to be totally courageous without hope in Heaven. Why risk your life if there is no hope that your story ends in anything other than worms and decay? Also, no one can be truly wise without faith, for faith sees higher and farther than reason or experience can. It sees "through a glass, dimly" but it sees deeply. Finally, no one can successfully practice self-control without God's grace, for we are all addicted to sin, self-indulgence, and selfishness.

The point is simply that without God's grace we cannot be good. Without love, justice turns to cruelty. Without hope, courage turns to blind despair. Without faith, this-worldly wisdom is foolishness to God. The two levels hang together.

Let us now look at the three greatest things in the world, as Saint Paul tells them in 1 Corinthians 13, keeping in mind only two simple questions: What is the essence of faith, of hope, of charity? and Why are they absolutely necessary?

FAITH

As Saint Paul argues in Romans, from the beginning faith was our justification with God. Tracing it back to Abraham (Romans 4), he could have traced it back to Eden. The Fall was first of all a fall of faith. First of all Eve believed the serpent when he told her she would not die if she ate the forbidden fruit, rather than believing God when He told her that she would. Only because of her lack of faith did she disobey. Faith or its lack is the root cause of obedience or disobedience, faithfulness or sin. Sin is faithlessness, infidelity.

Faith is first. But what is it? It is not mere belief, or mere trust, though it includes both. Belief is an intellectual matter (I believe the sun will shine tomorrow; I believe I am in good health; I believe the textbooks). Trust is an emotional matter (I trust my psychiatrist, or my surgeon, or my architect). Faith is more. It flows from the heart, the center of the person, the prefunctional root out of which both the intellectual and the emotional branches grow. Faith is the yea-saying, the commitment, of the I, the person.

The object of faith is God, not ideas about God. It is essential to know things about God, but it is more essential to know God.

Saint Thomas Aquinas, that most rational (not the same as rationalistic) of theologians, insists that "the object of the act of faith is not a proposition but a reality," God Himself. The Creed says, "I believe in God the Father Almighty, maker of heaven and earth." Just as the *object* of moral fidelity is not the law but the Lawgiver (law being a *description* of fidelity), so the object of faith is not the truths about God but the God who *is* Truth. The creedal truths about Him are a description of faith, a defining, a statement of its structure. The creeds are like accounting books, God is like the actual money.

Though the root of faith is not intellectual, its fruit is. "Faith seeking understanding," *fides quaerens intellectum*—this was the operative slogan for a thousand years of Christian philosophy. "Unless you believe, you will not understand"—faith first. But "in Thy light we see light"—understanding follows. How accurately the saints knew God; how mistaken the unbelieving geniuses!

Faith is more active than reason. Faith runs ahead of reason. Reason reports, like a camera. Faith takes a stand, like an army. Faith is saying yes to God's marriage proposal. Faith is extremely simple. Saying anything more would probably confuse it. Most of what is written about faith is needlessly complex. The word *yes* is the simplest word there is.

HOPE

Hope is the forgotten virtue in our time, for hope means hope for Heaven, and modernity's nose-to-the-grindstone, this-worldliness dares not lift its eyes to the open skies. Hope means that our heads do not bump up against the low ceiling of this world; hope means that the exhilarating, wonderful, and terrifying winds of Heaven blow in our ears.

More concretely, hope is faith directed to the future. God is the object of hope, just as God is the object of faith. Just as God's revelation, summarized in the Church's creeds, defines or expresses the structure of faith, so God's revelation, in the form of His many *promises* (there are over 300 promises in Scripture), defines or expresses the structure of hope. Neither faith nor hope is a vague, inchoate, subjective sentiment. Both are definite *responses,* affirmative responses, to God's initiative, God's revelation, God's very definite, specific, and verbal Word to us. It is not just "I believe" but "I believe God, the God revealed in Scripture, the God revealed in Christ." It is not just "I hope" but "I hope in God, the God revealed in Scripture; I hope for all the promises God has given us."

"I hope" has been terribly trivialized today, just as "I believe" has. "I believe" often means merely "I am of the opinion," and "I hope" often means merely "I wish," or "I would like it if . . ." However Christian hope is *certain,* "in the sure and certain hope of the Resurrection." God's promises *will* come true; there is no *if, and,* or *but* about it. For God is Truth itself.

The scriptural notion of truth is not an abstract, static, and timeless formula, but is something that comes true in time as the fulfillment of a divine promise. Truth *happens* in history. How dramatic!

French author Gabriel Marcel defines hope as the "affirmation that beyond all data, all inventories, and all calculations there exists a mysterious principle [*principium,* "origin," not "abstract statement" or "formula"] which is in connivance with me, which cannot but will that which I will if what I will deserves to be willed and is in fact willed with the whole of my being."[1] Hope means that my deepest values, wants, demands, longings, and ideals are not meaningless subjective blips on my inner mental sea but are like radar, an indication of objective reality. Hope means that when I cannot but choose life, the reason is that at the heart of reality, life is chosen. Hope means that when I say that it is better

to be than not to be, my very existence and the existence of everything that is joins me in a great universal chorus of approval.
Hope ultimately means that my implicit desire for God is God's
own trace in my being. Hope means that my agony and ecstasy of
longing for a joy this world can never give is a sure sign that I was
made for Him who is Joy, and Him alone.

LOVE

And now comes the greatest thing in the world, love. *Agapē* is
what is meant, of course, that new, specific, radical kind of love
that the world simply had not seen before Christ, not natural, human love. It is not *storge*, "affection," the love mothers naturally
have for babies, that pet owners have for pets, that natives have for
their native land, and that owners have for things owned. It is not
"liking." Also it is not *eros*, "desire," sexual or otherwise, for that
proceeds from need and from emptiness, while *agapē* proceeds
from fullness. It is not even *philia*, "friendship," the highest of human loves, the love praised by the ancients and forgotten by the
moderns.

No, *agapē* is the love that created the universe and sent Christ
down to suffer Hell on the cross to save us rebels, the love that
kissed the traitor Judas, suffered the soldiers' slaps and sneers, and
prayed, "Father, forgive them, for they know not what they do."
Was that love ever seen before Christ? Could that love ever be
confused with ordinary, humanly-attainable, natural loves?

It is true, as the Beatles said, that "all you need is love." But this
leaves the two crucial questions unanswered: What kind of love?
and even more important, How do you get it?

We need grace. We need God. We need to be loved despite our
sin. This is infinitely more than what secular psychology says, that
we need human positive strokes, that we are O.K. We are *not*
O.K., and we know it, even as we repeat, for the millionth time,

the most attractive lie the Devil has ever hooked us on, that we are intrinsically good. Modernized Christianity, in its desperate attempt to be accepted by the world, compromises its bad news of sin and thus trivializes its Good News of salvation. This modernized Christianity will never get what it wants, the world's acceptance, because even as it taunts us for our Puritanism, it respects us for telling the truth that it knows, deep down inside, it has covered up. The patient wants to be told by the nice doctor that there's nothing seriously wrong, but the patient knows all the time that both are fooling themselves. Dying people in America are usually told they're going to be just fine and they play along to spare the family the grief and honesty it cannot endure, thus plunging both into a conspiracy of lies. The same is true with regard to the greater illness of the spirit when we indulge in the conspiracy of lies that everything's going to be all right. That's the song people sing as they march to Hell.

We need God's love, not just man's. Man's love is fickle. Many of our marriages are lies and betrayals, with promises broken, pledged fidelities scorned, sacred vows sacrificed on the altar of the God of "I gotta be me." Even family bonds break. Nevertheless "when my mother and my father forsake me,/Then the LORD will take care of me" (Ps. 27:10). "Lord, to whom shall we go? You have the words of eternal life" (John 6:68).

Agapē must be supernatural because only God has no needs. Human love is not enough because it is always mixed, always flowing partly from need, from emptiness. We cannot build on a foundation that has holes; we cannot build on emptiness; and we are emptiness; we are need; we are a little child crying in the night.

If you want to know what *agapē* is, look at Christ dying for us on the cross. That is the best definition of love in the world. Saint Bernard of Clairvaux, the twelfth-century preacher, said that whenever he looked at a crucifix, he saw Christ's five wounds as lips speaking to him the words, "I love you."

Agapē is not mere pity, mere compassion. We hear a lot about compassion today, but compassion is not enough. A Hindu or a Buddhist practices compassion *(karuna),* but he leaves the dying in the street to fulfill his *karma,* and he regards Mother Teresa as an interfering busybody. *Agapē* is a busybody; it is active, demanding, and revolutionary. It is not feeling; it is action. For it is the nature of God, who is action, not feeling. Feelings are passive, passivities, passions, pushed around by wind, weather, digestion, heredity, environment, or whatever. God cannot be pushed around. God has no passions. God is infinite activity. His love is like the sun, like a billion burning suns.

The three theological virtues are a single plant. Faith is its root. Hope is its stalk, its life-thrust. Love is its fruit. The plant is God's own life in us. This is the "one thing necessary." Life offers us only one failure, to miss this, to miss God. Faith, hope, and charity are the hands that receive God.

CHAPTER SIX

The Beatitudes Confront the Seven Deadly Sins

The first psalm, the whole Psalter, in fact the whole Bible, teaches the blessedness of faith, hope, and charity and the misery of their opposites. There is bloom on the rose, there is reward, there is joy attached infallibly to this life, this way. No more perfect description of that joy exists than Jesus' Beatitudes, the beginning of the greatest and most famous sermon ever preached, the Sermon on the Mount. No better way exists to explore the blessedness of the life of supernatural virtue than to explore that sermon and the Beatitudes.

In this chapter we will discuss the proper interpretation of the sermon in light of Christian virtue, and the meaning of the word *beatitude*. Then, in the following chapters, we will look at each of the virtues set forth in the Beatitudes, and contrast them with the seven deadly sins, their opposites.

THE GREATEST SERMON EVER PREACHED

The greatest sermon ever preached takes only fifteen minutes to read and can be printed on a single page; yet it has changed the world more than any other speech ever made. Even Ghandi found nothing in his rich, six thousand-year-old Hindu tradition to equal it. Even atheists, agnostics, and humanists testify to its greatness. The whole world stares in an ecumenical orgy of agreement at it;

yet the whole world fails to *follow* it, exactly like the man in Jesus' parable at the end of the sermon (Matt. 7:24–27) who built his house on the sand of hearing instead of on the rock of heeding.

But before we can follow it, we must know it, and words can help to that end. My words, like those, are meant to be an arrow, not a target; a road map, not a journey; a laboratory manual, not an encyclopedia.

Matthew's version of the sermon takes three chapters (5–7), Luke's only one (6). Matthew probably compiled sayings spoken on various occasions into one, while Luke, who claims historical precision and order (1:3), probably reported the words in the order they were first spoken. The gist, structure, beginning and end of the sermon are the same in both accounts. Both begin with the Beatitudes, the gateway to all the rest. Matthew lists nine beatitudes, Luke four. Luke specifies four correlative woes to his four blessings, Matthew does not. Matthew specifies the spiritual nature of the beatitude of poverty and of hunger, Luke does not.

But what really matters, in the last analysis, is only three things: what the words mean, whether they are true, and what difference they make to me, to my life. That is true of all words, especially sermons, especially Jesus' sermons, and most especially this one.

The historical setting is important, however, because it helps us understand what Jesus meant. The wider setting is the history of Israel. Some interpreters seem to forget that Jesus was a Jew, neither a guru nor an angel. A Jew loves the law of God next to God Himself, for the Law is man's road to God, man's link to God, man's glue to God. The Law came from God through Moses, the greatest of all the prophets, the man with whom God spoke face to face (Deut. 34:10). Now Jesus, the new Moses, the greater-than-Moses, gives the new law for the new Kingdom, the thing symbolized and prepared for by the old. Thus Jesus also gives his law from a mountain, as did Moses. Matthew, who writes to Jews, mentions this detail; Luke, who writes to Gentiles, does not.

The immediate setting is described in Matthew 4:23–25. Jesus' reputation as teacher and healer had preceded him. "Great multitudes followed him," and the entire country was in an uproar, agog with hope or hate or simply astonishment over this man. The Greek word *thauma* ("wonder," "amazement") is used many times to characterize all three groups of hearers: disciples, enemies, and inquirers; believers, unbelievers, and agnostics.

Jesus is both healer and preacher; both teach. Jesus teaches by words and by deeds. The deeds (miracles) are also signs *(sēmeia)*, acted words. He had healed (Matt. 4:23–24), now He enlightens. Those who had received health now also receive truth. Both Jesus' healings and His preaching stem from the same source, His compassion on our need. It is upon "seeing the multitudes" (5:1), sheep without a shepherd, that He preaches this sermon.

WHAT DOES JESUS MEAN?

Five different interpretations of the sermon depend on five different solutions to its major problem, which is that we simply cannot practice these most practical words. They are meant to be heeded, not just heard (7:21–27); yet though we hear them, we do not and, it seems, cannot heed them. Its ideal is simply too high for human nature, like the stars that are, as Machiavelli says, beautiful but remote, too distant to enlighten earthly paths.

One solution is Albert Schweitzer's idea that Jesus' teachings could be practiced if and only if we believe that His second coming is imminent. This sermon is seen as an "interim ethic," a kind of holding pattern before the end of the world. Thus it is viable only for the first generation of Christians, who expected to be also the last. In plain terms, its practicability is based on an illusion; it is practically true only if theoretically false. Not only is this interpretation irreverent, it is also irrelevant to us, and in fact logically self-contradictory. How can truth be based on falsehood?

A second solution is to eschatologize it, to interpret its ideals as predictions that are livable only in heaven after death, or perhaps on earth only in the Millennium, the thousand-year-long earthly kingdom to be established by Christ after His second coming according to a literalist interpretation of Revelation 20. This "solution" effectively removes its bark from our ears because it removes its bite from our lives, and from those Jesus addressed in the first place. It says in effect that Jesus fed the hungry multitudes with frozen food that could not be thawed until Heaven, food we could not bite into until we got unearthly teeth in the next life. It freezes Jesus' fire in a time capsule.

A third solution is an elitist one, for it sees Jesus' directions not as commands or expectations for ordinary Christians but as counsels for extraordinary Christians, as a description of heroic sanctity. The traditional Catholic distinction between commands and counsels can be overdone and misunderstood and lead to this elitism. This misunderstanding was rightly rejected by the Protestant reformers, who here followed the ancient Fathers of the Church. The elitist interpretation also removes Jesus' bite from us, and ignores the fact that Jesus' audience was not made up of supersaints but of sinners like ourselves.

A fourth solution is that of the modern Left which interprets the sermon as a utopian social blueprint, like Plato's *Republic,* Lao Tzu's *Tao Te Ching,* or Rousseau's *Emile,* as the prescriptions for an enlightened, peaceful, and happy society. This interpretation naively assumes what all of history disproves, that we broken bricks can constitute an unbroken building if only we have an unbroken blueprint. Malcolm Muggeridge says, more realistically, that the most unpopular of all Christian dogmas is the one that is most empirically verifiable, the dogma of Original Sin.

The fifth and remaining interpretation is the one that naturally emerges from the text, that the sermon is for us, for all, for our individual lives here and now, however hard it is. But what then of the puzzle? What of its hardness, its impracticability?

To solve our puzzle, let us return to interpretation four, the liberal-humanist-socialist interpretation and look more closely at what is mistaken about it, for this mistake will lead us by contrast to the truth that solves our puzzle.

According to the theological liberal, this sermon is the essence of Christianity, and Christ is the best of human teachers and examples. But He is not divine, for His function is a human one, to teach and exemplify ethics. Christianity is essentially ethics.

What's missing here? Simply, it is the essence of Christianity, which is *not* the Sermon on the Mount. When Christianity was proclaimed throughout the world, the proclamation *(kerygma)* was not "Love your enemies!" but "Christ is risen!" This was not a new ideal but a new event, that God became man, died, and rose for our salvation. Christianity is first of all not ideal but real, an event, news, the gospel, which is "good news." The essence of Christianity is not Christianity; the essence of Christianity is Christ.

Even Christ's exalted ethical teaching in this sermon is not wholly unique. One can find equivalents or near-equivalents for nearly everything here in some of the rabbis, and in Socrates, Solomon, Buddha, Confucius, and Lao Tzu. These profound men intuited from afar something of the high goal we are called to; but they did not know the way. Jesus not only knew the way but *was* the Way. He did not say, like Buddha, "Look not to me, look to my teaching *(dharma)*." He said the exact opposite: "I am the way. . . . No one comes to the Father except through Me" (John 14:6). Jesus is a teacher, and the best One, although not the only One. However, He is the only Way, the only Savior, the only Jesus.

Yet although Jesus' ethical teachings in this sermon are not the essence of Christianity, they are essentially connected with it. The essence is Christ, Christ-for-us, our New Birth in Christ. But new birth is followed by new life, and this sermon describes that new life. Children's lives resemble their parents'; and when we become children of God by faith and baptism, we begin to resemble Him and our lives begin to resemble His life.

Humanism tries to imitate the effect without acquiring the cause. It can't be done; you can't get blood from a stone. So humanism must either despair of attaining the effect (the first three interpretations) or water down its difficulty (the fourth). For we are simply unable to live this divine life by human power. The only way to "the imitation of Christ" is the incorporation into Christ; the only way to be *like* Christ is to *be* Christ. Only Christ can live Christian ethics. But He lives it in His body as well as in Himself as our head. "Without me you can do nothing," He says; but his apostle says, "I can do all things through Christ who strengthens me."

The sermon, like 1 Corinthians 13, describes *agapē*. *Agapē* is the nature of God (God is *agapē*), but not the nature of fallen man. It is profoundly true that "all you need is love," but the kind of love you need is not mere human need-love but divine bounty, *agapē,* and that cannot come from a merely human source. Even if humanism overcomes the first illusion and perceives the radical difference between human and divine love, it does not know how to get it. Nowhere in the Bible do we find the humanist's prescription of "try a little harder." Man's answer is "try," God's is "trust." Faith alone opens the door of the soul to the divine lover who impregnates it with His own life. The Sermon on the Mount describes that life, the fruits of faith. Humanism tries to grow the fruit without the root.

THE LAW OF CHRIST

I believe Luther and Barth are at least partially correct, in fact profoundly so, when they interpret this sermon as what a Zen Buddhist would call a *koan,* an unsolvable puzzle, meant not to fill but to empty ourselves, to teach us our impotence. This seems to be Pauline theology. The Law, he says, was our pedagogue, our schoolmaster, to bring us to Christ. Christ does not bring us to the Law, the Law brings us to Christ; it is our diagnosis and Christ is our cure. Christ himself says in this sermon that his teaching is not a new, alien law, but the fulfillment of the old one. Therefore it must fulfill the purpose of the old Law even more strongly than the old Law itself. That purpose is not the good news but the bad news, not the cure but the diagnosis. Therefore the new law's demands are more difficult, not less. Jesus does not liberalize the Law; he tightens it. We must avoid not only murder, but hate; not only adultery, but lust. We must not only stop slapping cheeks but offer our own to be slapped.

The Mosaic Law simply cannot be obeyed by human nature unless it is misinterpreted pharisaically, externally. Jesus' spiritual and interior interpretation of the Law is not new; the pharisaic interpretation was new. Jesus did not soften the Law; the Pharisees softened the Law. They were the liberals, not Jesus. Listen to their demands and you may go home thinking "Thank you, Lord, that I am a good person." However when you listen to Jesus' sermon, you cry out "God be merciful to me, a sinner." It shows us our scabs and sends us screaming to the Savior. Anyone who hears it and goes home with a satisfied smile on his face is simply an egregious ass.

Further evidence that Jesus uses the Law as a *koan* is the incident with the rich young ruler (Matt. 19:16–26), who had obeyed the commandments perfectly from his youth. Jesus does not say to him, "Welcome to my Kingdom; you have qualified." Instead, He erects another, higher, and harder law atop the old one that the young man had surmounted. "Sell what you have and give to the poor . . . and come, follow Me." Jesus knew he could not do that. He went away sorrowful. Jesus sounds cruel here, but He is really kind. The sorrow that precedes repentence is necessary. Jesus showed the young man his need, his sin, which was a cancer so deeply seated that the old Law, especially if externally interpreted, had not revealed it. He had passed his X-ray test, but Jesus ordered a CAT scan, and the patient went away sorrowful because now he knew he needed an operation.

We all need Jesus' operation, and before the Wounded Surgeon tells us the good news of His healing, He tells us the bad news of our disease. Sin and salvation, bad news and good, repentance and faith, disease and cure—these are the inseparable parts of Jesus' teaching, and that of all the prophets. If the first does not stand, neither does the second. "Those who are well have no need of a physician, but those who are sick" (Matt. 9:12).

The Sermon on the Mount not only comes from Jesus but also leads us to Jesus. It does not divert us from Jesus to a set of abstract ideals, but its ideals lead us to Jesus, who alone can fulfill them in us, if we let Him. The sermon is an arrow, and Jesus is the bull's eye, not vice versa.

WHAT IS "BEATITUDE"?

The gateway to the Sermon on the Mount is the Beatitudes. They are God's answer to man's greatest question. Blessedness, beatitude, is what all of us are seeking all the time *in* and *by* everything we seek. Blessedness is always our end, whether our means is pleasure or power or riches or virtue or wisdom or honor or anything else. Blessedness is the *summum bonum,* "the greatest good." Everyone seeks it, but not everyone finds it, because not everyone knows where it is. Saint Augustine says, "Seek what you seek, but it is not where you seek it." Not everyone has a road map. Jesus here gives us the road map for our lives. This is the greatest of all treasure maps to the greatest of all treasures, and it is given to us absolutely free. It has to be a gift, for we would never have found life's most precious treasure on our own. Proof of this is the fact that the Beatitudes are shocking to us. They come like great jets of flame from the divine fire, solar storms on the surface of the sun of God.

The treasure they point us to is not just *happiness,* but *blessedness.* Some modern versions of the Bible translate the word *makarios* as "happy." This is a fundamental and disastrous mistake. For *happy* means to the modern reader something subjective, a state of consciousness, a feeling. If you feel happy, you are happy. It also connotes a temporary state, and something dependent on fortune (*hap* is the Old English word for "fortune" or "chance"). *Blessedness,* on the other hand, is an objective state, not a subjective feeling. So we can be mistaken about it, in fact, most of the world is. That's why Jesus has to teach us, even shock us. Blessedness is also a permanent state and dependent on God's grace and our choice, neither chance nor fortune.

Suffering is the crucial test separating happiness from blessedness. Suffering can be part of blessedness, but not part of happiness. Job is not *happy* there on his dung heap scratching his boils with a potsherd, deprived of family and fortune, blamed by wife and friends, seemingly forsaken by God. What arrogant nonsense to tell Job he is happy! But he *is* blessed, though he does not know it, because he is learning wisdom and coming closer to God, his true good, his true blessedness. It is startling to tell mourners they are blessed, but it is simply silly to tell them they are happy.

The typically modern mind is much more subjectivistic than the premodern mind. It seeks happiness rather than blessedness, feeling rather than fact. Thus its relativistic slogan is: "Happiness is . . . different things to different people." The response of the modern mind to the Beatitudes is: "Well, that may be O.K. for you, but not for me. For me, happiness is a warm puppy." Within horizons bounded by subjective feeling, no one is ever wrong because no one is ever right. It is indeed a warm, puppyish world. By contrast, Jesus is like a glacier, or an explosion, or the blast of a trumpet from heaven. As Matthew notes at the end of his sermon, "When Jesus had ended these sayings, . . . the people were astonished at His teaching, for He taught them as one having authority, and not as the scribes" (7:28-29). Happy feelings do not astonish, but objective reality often does. Jesus offers us a plunge into the breathtakingly steep mountains and gorges of reality.

A GLORIOUS PARADOX

Each of the Beatitudes is an outrageous paradox. Those whom worldly wisdom regards as the least blessed turn out to be the most blessed, and vice versa. Apparent losers are real winners, apparent winners are real losers. There is a staggering contrast between appearance and reality. No one can read these beatitudes without his spirit staggering, unless it is already flat on its back asleep. Preachers and teachers are tempted to mitigate the scandal and prop up the staggering spirit for the sake of good feelings and acceptability, something Jesus never did. In fact, He seems to have done the opposite, making His teaching as uncompromising as possible to separate clearly the sheep from the goats.

Many preachers try to make Christianity in general and the Beatitudes in particular *acceptable*—that key word of modern ethics. Behavior must be "acceptable" or "appropriate" rather than "good" or "right" or (heaven help us!) "virtuous" or (most unthinkable of all) "holy." For if we are acceptable, the world will accept us. And isn't that the Church's business, to win the world, to get its message accepted?

No, it is not.

Jesus commanded us not to succeed, but to obey; not to sell the gospel, but to proclaim it. Jesus was not found "acceptable"; He was nailed to a cross. And He told his disciples to expect the same kind of reaction, for human nature *will* not change and the proclamation of the gospel *should* not change. It is not our job to convert the world or to fill churches; that is God's job. Ours is to sow the seed, without sugar-coating it; God's is to make it take root and grow.

The apparent kindness of the preachers who water down Jesus' hard sayings is really arrogance. They are like mail carriers who arrogate to themselves the role of editors of the mail that is entrusted to them to deliver intact. Some preachers act as if Jesus had said, "Blessed are you when all men speak well of you." But the real Jesus said, "Woe to you when all men speak well of you, For so did their fathers to the false prophets" (Luke 6:26). If we never offend anyone, we are not giving them Jesus.

Jesus *must* offend us, for He tells us not what we want to hear but what we need to hear, and sin has inserted a great gap between our needs and our wants. Jesus must surprise us, for He comes from Heaven; how could Heaven not surprise earth? Earth's ethical teachers give us what comes from the human heart—fairly familiar territory. The Man from Heaven tells us what "eye has not seen, nor ear heard, nor have entered into the heart of man" (1 Cor. 2:9). Most of our ethical teachers give us either old platitudes or new nonsense, safe old truths or dangerous new lies. Confucius is a good example of the former, Nietzsche of the latter. The first type is reliable but dull, the other fascinating but deranged. Jesus is wholly different. He gives us neither old orthodoxies nor new heresies, but the very mind of God, fresh water springing straight from the glacier of God's heavenly mountain, refreshing the soul and welling up with eternal life. This is the reason that His words are literally inexhaustible. They are so simple that a child can understand them, yet so profound that no sage can exhaust them. They are like a face that way. They *are* a face: God's face, God's will, God's personality.

The Beatitudes are part of the gospel, the good news. They are surprising because they are news, but they are beatitudes because they are good news—to the poor, the meek, the mourners. But they are bad news to the rich, the arrogant, the comfortable. It is not hard to see why. Jesus came to establish a new kingdom, the kingdom of heaven. It threatens the sovereignty of the old kingdom, the kingdom of this world. To enter Jesus' kingdom, we must abandon our old allegiance. Naturally that act of treason to the "prince of this world" will be most difficult for those who have most to lose by the trade, those most addicted to the delights of this world. Jesus never says riches are evil, but He says many times and with great force that riches make it very *hard* to enter His kingdom. His meaning is unmistakable, simple and clear, and quite "unacceptable."

The double-edged character of the Beatitudes is clear in Luke's account; but even in Matthew's account it can be said that seven of the nine Beatitudes are the opposites to the seven deadly sins. The poor in spirit, who are detached from riches, are the opposite of the avaricious, who are addicted to them. Those who mourn, who are empty of pleasure, are the opposite of the gluttonous, who are filled with pleasures. The meek are the opposite of the proud. Those who hunger and thirst for righteousness are the opposite of the slothful, who lack spiritual ambition. The pure in heart are the opposite of the lustful. The peacemakers are the opposite of the wrathful. And those who are persecuted for righteousness' sake, that is, those who are willing to suffer for good, are the opposite of the envious who are unwilling to have less satisfaction or more suffering than others. The Beatitudes are a job description for "doorkeeper in the House of God"; their opposites are for "dwelling in the tents of wickedness." And the shocking thing is that these are the only two jobs in town.

AN INTERLOCKING

Each of the Beatitudes, like an island in an archipelago, is connected to each of the others below the surface. Each is an outcropping of the same massive undersea mountain. Thus an explorer in the deeps of the spirit, like a diver, can find the connecting bridges and the underlying unity. That unity is Christ Himself, His life, the new existence He brought into the world which He calls "the kingdom of God" or "the kingdom of Heaven," the new life He invites us to enter by faith and baptism. (It is, remember, not just a new *lifestyle* but a new *life*. It is just as real as a continent, for the New Birth is just as real and just as new as the old birth.)

The bridges are easy to find.

For example, the poor in spirit, those detached from the desire for worldly goods, must necessarily also be the pure in heart, since their heart is not split and set on the many things of this world, but purely on the one thing necessary. They love God and therefore they shall see God. These pure in heart, in turn, are the meek, the holy and harmless and humble, because that is the character of the God their hearts are set on. The meek, in turn, are persecuted by the world and made to mourn; they are taken advantage of. Yet by their very act of suffering persecution they are the peacemakers. They make peace by the same method Christ did on the cross, by draining off the bloody mess of human history into their own broken hearts. The peacemakers are also the merciful, for war is caused by the insistence on justice almost as much as by injustice. The cure for war and the way to peace is not justice but mercy, forgiveness. Yet the merciful hunger and thirst for justice even as they go beyond it to mercy, for they realize that in God's spiritual economic recovery program for our fallen world the only way to justice is not from below, from force, from something less than justice (like bombs) but from above, from something more than justice, from mercy, from the character of God Himself as revealed in Christ. It is Christ's mercy in dying for us that satisfies justice. Mercy and truth met together, righteousness and peace have kissed each other on the Cross.

This string of thought holding together the pearls of the Beatitudes is only one of many, selected at random. Each beatitude is connected with and implies every other one. There are myriads of undersea bridges linking these islands.

THE SEVEN DEADLY SINS

Just as the Beatitudes summarize the blessedness of supernatural virtue, the seven deadly sins summarize the misery of supernatural vice. Unlike the Beatitudes, the seven deadly sins are not found together in Scripture as such, but they are all warned against in Scripture. Centuries of experience tell us to avoid them.

We understand things best by contrast. Thus we understand supernatural virtue best by contrast with supernatural vice. For there is a close parallel between the vices and virtues, as follows:

VICES (Seven Deadly Sins)	VIRTUES (Beatitudes)
Pride	Poverty of spirit (humility)
Avarice (greed)	Mercy
Envy	Mourning
Wrath	Meekness and peacemaking
Sloth	Hunger and thirst for righteousness
Lust	Purity of heart
Gluttony	Persecution

FIGURE 6

Pride is self-assertion, selfishness; poverty of spirit is humility, selflessness.

Avarice is greed, the centrifugal reach to grab and keep the world's goods for oneself; mercy is the centripetal reach to give, to share the world's goods with others, even the undeserving.

Envy resents another's happiness; mourning shares another's unhappiness.

Wrath wills harm and destruction; meekness refuses to harm and peacemaking prevents destruction.

Sloth refuses to exert the will toward the good, toward the ideal; hunger and thirst for righteousness does just that.

Lust dissipates and divides the soul, desiring every attractive body; purity of heart centers and unifies the soul, desiring God alone.

Gluttony needs to consume an inordinate amount of worldly goods; being persecuted is being deprived of even ordinate necessities.

THE SOURCE OF THE SEVEN DEADLY SINS

The Beatitudes come from Heaven. They are preached by the God-Man who came from Heaven. But where do the seven deadly sins come from?

I had a dream once that answered that question. It was a dream with terrific potential for terror, but I felt no terror at all; it just registered, like a computer printout. I think God sent it to me in that spirit: all business, no nonsense, "just the facts, sir."

I saw an incredibly deep chasm, a pit or abyss, walled round vaguely with massive confining walls. The riveting thing about it was its depth. I was standing on a platform which reached out into the abyss, and from miles below there came up two pale blue jets of fire. They reached all the way up to my level without diminishment, like laser beams, but they quivered like flames from a gas oven. Straight up they shot, unhampered.

Then I saw a long wire handle, like an enormous barbecue skewer, extended out over the pit. At the end of the handle there was an enclosed cage, or cave, or cocoon. Some creature was inside, being roasted over the flames. After a few minutes smoke began coming out of the cage. Then it was withdrawn from the abyss and the flame, to a solid platform, and opened.

Out came, to my astonishment, a little girl. She was unconscious and smouldering. "Is she dead?" I asked. But I understood somehow that she was not. Incredibly, she had survived the ordeal, but just barely. She was smoking like a burnt hamburger over charcoal.

Then I awoke, and I think I understood. Hell's fires reach into our lives, undiminished by material distance. All sins, especially the deadly sins, ultimately come from one place, from Hell. God's commandments, God's directions, God's morality for us are not just for better relations with each other, but are also for escaping the flames and their work even at a distance. God knows where the flames are; we often do not. In that tissue of mysteries that is our lives, His road map alone is infallible, and it points out the spaces that are safe from the flames.

The smallest sin is a small spark from the one fire that is Hellfire. All sin is from Hell. If it were not, it would not be absolutely forbidden. It is said that there are three sources of evil, "the world, the flesh, and the Devil"; but the world and the flesh would be innocent were it not for the Devil.

All evil is from Hell. Where else could it be from? From God? From any good thing God made? From the goodness in us that He made? The world and ourselves become evil only by being held over the flames.

But the vision is not a pessimistic, doomsday one. The little girl was saved in the end. The point of the vision, I think, is watchfulness. She was saved only barely. A few more minutes of the flame and she would have died. No one knows how long a human soul can endure the flames of sin before it dies; no one knows when in any individual case venial sin becomes mortal sin, just as no one knows whether a certain pagan has the implicit love of God in his heart even before the gospel is preached to him, and so he is saved. And because no one knows, in both cases, we must shout with a loud and prophetic voice. Because the liberal is right about us not knowing who is saved, therefore the fundamentalist is right about the need for clear warnings against sin and Hell and calls to be saved. The fundamentalist conclusion (which is simply the Christian conclusion) follows from the liberal premise.

Only after the dream was over did I realize that I had seen only one hand holding the skewer out over the flames but two hands bringing it back. "Without Me you can do nothing," God says. But He also says to us, "Without you I will do nothing." He wants the free choice of our hearts, not passivity, in running our race from misery to beatitude.

We begin our contrast between the seven deadly sins and the Beatitudes by contrasting the first and foundational sin, pride, with the first and foundational virtue, humility, or poverty of spirit.

CHAPTER SEVEN

Poor in Spirit vs. Proud at Heart

PRIDE

Aristotle called it one of the virtues. Christianity calls it the greatest of all vices. Nothing distinguishes Christian morality from pagan morality more sharply than their opposite attitudes toward pride.

C. S. Lewis wrote:

> There is one vice of which no man in the world is free; which every one in the world loathes when he sees it in someone else; and of which hardly any people except Christians ever imagine that they are guilty themselves. . . . There is no fault which makes a man more unpopular, and no fault which we are more unconscious of in ourselves. And the more we have it ourselves, the more we dislike it in others.[1]

pride

Pride is the greatest sin. It comes not from the world or the flesh but from the Devil. It comes from Hell. It was the Devil's original sin, perhaps the only sin possible for a pure spirit. (Hell's work is purely spiritual, you know; Hell cannot produce a single atom of that blessed creation of God, matter.)

Pride was also Adam's (our) original sin, the desire to be like God, over the Law rather than under it.

It is the first and greatest sin because it is the violation of the first

95

and greatest commandment, "You shall have no other gods before Me." Pride puts self before God. Pride loves the self with all your heart and soul and mind and strength rather than God.

Saint Augustine says in *The City of God* that everyone in the world belongs to one of two cities: the City of God, which consists of "all who love God to the despising of self," and the city of the world, who "love self to the despising of God." (Remember no man can serve two masters.) God is the source, the life-blood, and heavenly End of the first city, the devil of the second. That is the cosmic difference between humility and pride.

C. S. Lewis encapsulates Augustine's essential point in *The Great Divorce:* "There are only two kinds of people, in the end: those who say to God, 'Thy will be done' and those to whom God says, in the end, '*thy* will be done.'"

This is what theologian Karl Rahner calls everyone's "fundamental option," being for or against God, however imperfectly known. God is a gentleman and respects our fundamental choice—eternally.

Pride is the greatest sin because it is the living heart of all sins. Every sin says to God, "*my* will be done."

Pride excludes not only God but also neighbor, Christ's body as well as Christ. For there can be only one Number One. Pride is essentially competitive.

Non-Christians think so little about pride's sinfulness that they frequently appeal to pride to eradicate other vices. Parents and teachers often appeal to a child's pride and self-respect to turn him from lust, cheating, or bad temper. I have even heard priests in the confessional well-intentionedly use this appeal.

God uses exactly the opposite technique, as pointed out in the *Summa* (II-II, 162, 6 ad 3) by Saint Thomas (who was, incidentally, a master of practical spirituality as well as speculative theology):

In order to overcome their pride, God punishes certain men by allowing them to fall into sins of the flesh, which though they be less grievous are more evidently shameful. . . . From this indeed the gravity of pride is made manifest. For just as a wise physician, in order to cure a worse disease, allows the patient to contract one that is less dangerous, so the sin of pride is shown to be more grievous by the very fact that, as a remedy, God allows men to fall into other sins.

Perhaps that is the reason why in God's providence there are so many priests and monks who are alcoholics or homosexuals.

Have you often wondered why God does not give you more grace, as He certainly could, to avoid your many sins? Well, now you know. And you also know how to receive that grace, through eradicating the thing that blocks it, your pride. That is why Saint Bernard of Clairvaux, when asked what the four cardinal virtues were, replied, "Humility, humility, humility, and humility." If you think you have gotten beyond this single-minded beginning, you are proud; in other words, you have *not* gotten beyond it.

If you think you are not in serious danger from your sin of pride, then you certainly are. If you are even a little proud of your humility, you are terribly proud indeed.

Socrates, humblest and wisest of philosophers, was told by the oracle that no one in the world was wiser than he. He proved this true by interpreting it to mean that neither he nor any other man was wise—"God alone is wise"—but that he alone knew that he was not wise, "and this is the only wisdom I or any other man can have." In other words, there are only two kinds of people, fools, who think they are wise, and the wise, who know they are fools. Augustine's two cities are the proud, who think they are humble, and the humble, who know they are proud. The only way to become humble is to admit you are proud.

Pride is not the same as vanity. In fact vanity, though it is a sin, shows some humility. For if I think I need your admiration, then I do not feel wholly independent of you, above you. The truly proud person couldn't care less what others think of him.

Pride is not first of all thinking too highly of yourself, because it isn't *thinking* first of all but *willing,* just as humility isn't thinking about yourself in a low way but not thinking of yourself at all. It's thinking less *about* yourself, not thinking less *of* yourself. Pride is willful arrogance, arrogating to yourself what is really God's.

Pride is not pleasure in being praised, wanting to please others (parents, friends, God). That too shows humility. The exemplars of pride are not movie stars but dictators.

Pride is essentially a lust for power, and this is far more widespread than dictators. It goes deeper even than the lust for pleasure, for we are willing to endure pains if only we are in control, in power, but not if we are not. Kierkegaard said, "If I had a humble servant who, when I asked him for a glass of water brought me instead the world's costliest wines blended in a chalice, I would dismiss him—to teach him that true pleasure consists in getting my own way."[2]

The song they all sing in Hell is the hymn to pride, "I Did It My Way," or the song Milton has Satan sing, "Better to reign in Hell than serve in Heaven." The song they all sing in Heaven is the hymn of humility, King David's song, "I would rather be a doorkeeper in the house of my God than dwell in the tents of wickedness."

But power is the new *summum bonum,* the new ideal of our Western civilization. Ever since the dawn of the modern era in the Renaissance (i.e., the Regression) and the Enlightenment (i.e., the Darkening), our civilization has been redirecting more and more of its spiritual interest and energy away from the traditional goal of conforming the soul to God and to the new goal of conforming the world to the desires of the soul, away from "Thy will be done" to "our will be done," from playing creature to playing God, from humility to pride. How many of us in the civilization dedicated to "man's conquest of nature" can even comprehend, must less applaud, C. S. Lewis' remark, "I was not born to be free. I was born to adore and to obey"?

Our civilization's fundamental goal is one of pride: It is Faustian, Promethean. The Tower of Babel is its perfect emblem. This is one of the reasons why Tolkien's *The Lord of the Rings* holds such a fascination for us. It questions our basic symbol, the Ring of Power, our new god.

I hope and pray that our fate follows that of Babel, not Faust, for Babel was a failure, and therefore hope remained. Faust was a success and was damned. Better God's failure than the world's success. Better God's black sheep than the world's hero. Rather the repentant prodigal than his proud elder brother. Rather the publican than the Pharisee.

The modern villain is not physics but psychology. Nearly all our modern psychologies tell us how to be "adult," "mature," and "responsible for our own lives." When you see these ubiquitous code words in catechism textbooks or sex education programs or religious education courses, remember what they are: the old paganism in new dress. Remember what *adult* suggests in our culture. Remember what *adult* books, magazines, and movies are like. Remember that Jesus *never* told us to be "adult" but instead said, "Unless you . . . become as little children, you will by no means enter the kingdom of heaven" (Matt. 18:3). Heaven's gate is too tiny for any but a child. It is the eye of a needle. Large adult camels must go home to die or be born again as little children.

We can easily update and apply what Pope Gregory the Great said in his *Moralia:*

There are four marks by which every kind of pride of the arrogant betrays itself: either when they think that their good is from themselves [humanism], or if they believe it to be from above yet they think that it is due to their own merits [Pelagianism, which still survives among many], or when they boast of having what they have not [e.g., well-integrated, mature, adult personalities], or despise others [e.g., the past, or simple, unprogressive people] and wish to appear the exclusive possessors of what they have.

The modern version of pride, though, is not usually aristocratic but egalitarian. This deludes us into thinking it is not pride at all. However even sheepish conformists can be collectively proud. Even though our passions are sleepy and our spirits lukewarm, that very sleepiness and refusal of awe, wonder, worship, and transcendent passion is a proud insult to God that He hates even more than rebellion: "I could wish you were cold or hot. . . . Because you are lukewarm, . . . I will spew you out of My mouth" (Rev. 3:16).

The deepest reason God hates pride, the reason pride is so hellish, is that it keeps us from knowing God, our supreme joy. Pride looks down, and no one can see God but by looking up.

Our supreme joy is simply being in God's presence; and in that presence we are necessarily humble. When we see God—the real God, not the comfortable chum of our updated catechisms—we see ourselves as Isaiah did: "Woe is me, for I am undone!/Because I am a man of unclean lips,/And I dwell in the midst of a people of unclean lips;/For my eyes have seen the King,/The LORD of hosts" (Isa. 6:5).

Better yet, we see ourselves less and less and God more and more. Ultimately, as the mystics say, we see ourselves not at all. God is all and we are nothing. This is our supreme joy.

Pride has ingrown eyeballs. Humility stares outward in self-forgetful ecstasy (*ek-stasis*, "standing-outside-yourself"). The God who loves us with an everlasting love is infinitely determined to bring us to that point, the consummation of the spiritual marriage. It is to make that moment possible that He trains us in humility. We must be stripped of all our frumpery and fancy dress for the naked embrace of the Spirit. Humility is the very life of Heaven. Pride is the frigidity of Hell.

> **"Blessed are the poor in spirit,**
> **for theirs is the kingdom of heaven."**

The opponent of pride is not despair but humility, or poverty of spirit. Pride and despair are twin brothers. They do not exclude each other but they encourage each other. There is a secret pride in despair—a tragic grandeur, an overweening claim unfulfilled—and a secret despair at being human in pride's demand to play God.

Humility is the opponent of both. It keeps us from despair as well as from pride. The greatest virtue keeps us from the greatest vice.

It is the greatest virtue in the sense that it is the first and foundational virtue. It is not the finest fruit of virtue—love is that—but it is the root. Just as the first of the Ten Commandments includes and implies all the others, so this first beatitude is the Key West of the keys to the Kingdom, the Big Island in the chain. It tells us the first prerequisite for membership in Christ's kingdom.

That prerequisite is escape from our present captivity to the kingdom of this world and to its riches, from its sway over our souls. This world, though created by God and declared "very good," fell when Adam, its priest, fell. After all, Scripture does not call *God* "the prince of this world!"

Our only two options are membership in either Satan's kingdom or God's kingdom. "No one can serve two masters." "He who is not with Me is against Me." Since membership is decided by the heart's allegiance, our first duty is detachment, poverty of spirit, dissolving the spiritual glue that glued us to Satan's kingdom so that we are free to belong to Christ. The glue is pride and its children, greed or avarice. The solvent is poverty of spirit, humility, willing to be poor in the riches of the world, or detachment.

The world from which we must be detached, the world that is Satan's kingdom, is not the planet, not matter, but our own greed and lust for it. "World" in the New Testament is *aiōn*. It is a time word, not a space word. It means "the old order," "the fallen order," "the Adam order." Christ has invaded that kingdom, that order. Christmas was D-day. We are liberated and called forever away from the old order.

Looking at what poverty of spirit does *not* mean helps us understand what it does mean. Nietzsche, like all unbelievers, can be helpful to believers here, for all misunderstandings can serve to clarify the truth, by contrast. Nietzsche says Jesus sided with the poor and weak because He Himself was weak, in spirit if not in body. The ancient vitality of the blood lines of the great kings, Saul, David, and Solomon, had become anemic. Jesus was delicate, decadent, sensitive, and high strung. He sided with underlings because he was one Himself. Resenting the strong, He seduced them to give up their strength and adopt His weakness. Christians have done the same ever since.

Now not only is this blasphemous but more to our point, it is inaccurate. It can be answered with a counter-question: Is strength to be measured by the standard of the bully?

"The poor in spirit" does *not* mean "the weak-spirited"! That is the misunderstanding of much of the world, and it is disastrous. It admires Jesus' goodness, but thinks of Him and His followers as noble sissies. Thinking goodness is weak and power amoral tragically separates goodness and power. Once that tragic separation opens up, there are only three options: immoralism and pragmatism, "the will to power" (Nietzsche); siding with the weak, identifying Christianity with niceness, peace of mind, sweetness and light, thus adding fuel to the fire of Nietzsche's criticism; or an uneasy compromise, dancing clumsily between goodness and power, Sunday and Monday, church and world. Unless Jesus combines goodness and power, unless his poverty of spirit is strength and not weakness, we must become either degraded, deflated, or divided.

What Nietzsche and his followers fail to see is the paradoxical nature of Christian detachment from the doors to worldly powers and the riches that are their skeleton key. Detachment from the world and attachment to God brings the greatest riches and the greatest power. God has more power in one breath of His spirit than all the winds of war, all the nuclear bombs, all the energy of all the suns in all the galaxies, all the fury of Hell itself.

The objector to poverty of spirit fails to understand the power of emptiness. The power Jesus refers to on the spiritual level is the same power that makes bowls, windows, and rooms useful on the physical level. Fill them up and they become useless; you take away their potentiality, their possibility. That power makes motherhood great on the biological level; it is the empty womb that can generate life. So spiritually, our strength is our receptivity, our active passivity to God, our emptiness, our motherhood (to God we are all women). We must let God be God in us. If we come to God with empty hands, He will fill them. If we come with full hands, He finds no place to put Himself. It is our beggary, our receptivity, that is our hope.

Thus comes the stinging paradox of Christ's negative statements. A rich man can enter the Kingdom only as a camel can go through a needle's eye. The Needle's Eye gate in the Jerusalem wall was barely wide enough for a camel, but not for its baggage. Merchants had to unload all their saddlebags for inspection before entrance to Jerusalem. We must do the same at the gate of death because "you can't take it with you." It (worldly goods) dies forever. If we identify with them, if we stick to them with spiritual glue, then we die forever with them. Only if we free ourselves, dissolve the glue, can we be saved and enter the Holy City.

In *The Weight of Glory*, C. S. Lewis says that God appears to us like an uncle to a slum child playing with mudpies in the street, offering a vacation at the seaside, but we stick to our mudpies. We are too easily content. Poverty of spirit is not mediocrity and cheap contentment; it is exactly the opposite; it is detachment from the mudpies for love of the sea. The Buddhist and the Stoic and the "peace of mind addict" teach detachment for the sake of tranquillity or Nirvana, but the Christian wants to be unclothed with the world and the goods of the body and the body itself only to be reclothed with Heaven and the resurrection body. Christ opposes selfish desire only to replace it with unselfish desire, not with emptiness. We are to be spiritually poor only for the sake of becoming spiritually rich, detached from what we can own so that we can be attached in a different way to what we cannot own, detached from consuming so that we can be consumed by God.

In the Philippines, monkeys are caught by hollowing out coconuts and inserting sticky, aromatic candy to attract the monkeys, who put in their hands to grab the candy and can't get their fists out. They won't let go, even when their captors approach, and they end up as monkey stew. Jesus sees us as monkeys and tells us, Let go! It seems raving nonsense to the monkeys, but it is simple sense. Addicts see sense as nonsense and nonsense as sense. That's why Jesus' sayings seem hard and paradoxical to us. We are all addicts, like the monkeys; only the brand of candy differs. "A man is a slave to anything he cannot part with that is less than himself," said Scottish novelist George MacDonald.

Since detachment is the prerequisite to attachment, Jesus spoke more about this topic—letting go of money, riches, worldly goods—than any other. There was no room for Him in the inn the first time He came, and there is often no room for Him in our spiritual inns when He comes and knocks on our spiritual doors now. The hard thing we must do is to kick out the present tenants. Jesus knows this is difficult; that's why He talks so much about it, in such harsh language, and why He puts this beatitude first. We identify with these tenants of our hearts, so when we let them die we feel as if something in us dies. We don't like to die, but we must learn to die, to kill, even.

It is not cruelty but wisdom for God to insist on sacrifice, on shed blood and death. It symbolizes what has to happen in us. Prayer, for instance, is a kind of death, a rehearsal for death. In praying we die to ourselves, our wills, our ordinary consciousnesses and desires and concerns, even our ordinary world, and enter God's world, aligning our minds and wills with God's. We die to our time, we sacrifice our loaves and fishes to Him.

And He multiplies them.

CHAPTER EIGHT

Giving Mercy vs. Getting Things (Avarice)

AVARICE

Its old name was "covetousness." Its new name is "greed." Christian tradition ranks it even ahead of lust and second only to pride in the list of all-time spiritual villains. Saint Paul calls it "the root of all evil." It is avarice, the love of money, "the immoderate desire for temporal possessions which can be estimated in money," as Saint Thomas defined it in the *Summa*.

Money is ubiquitously tempting because of a kind of umbrella principle, covering everything money can buy. It also is (or rather falsely promises to be) a security blanket against change. It apes divine self-sufficiency.

Avarice is not desire as such, or even desire for temporal possessions as such, but the *immoderate* desire for them; for it is natural to man to desire external things *as means,* but avarice makes them into ends, into gods. And when a creature is made into a god, it becomes a devil.

However, creatures are good in themselves. In a biblical, creationist world-view, *things* are good, *all* things are good, *being* as such is good *(ens est bonum)*. There are only two categories of being. All being is either the supremely good Creator or else His creation, which He Himself solemnly pronounced "very good" after creating it. Nevertheless fallen man worshiped and served the creature rather than the Creator. "In this sense," says Saint Thomas, "covetousness is the root of all sin . . . as every sin grows out of the love of temporal things . . . [and] every sin includes an inordinate turning to a mutable good."

God seems to have considered avarice especially important as early as Moses' time, for the only two of the Ten Commandments that deal explicitly with inner attitudes of spirit rather than outer actions are the ninth and tenth, which forbid avarice. ("Thou shalt not covet. . . .")

Jesus spoke more about avarice than about any other sin. Just count the times He talked about money—"riches," "possessions," "mammon." His attention, unlike ours, was not fixated on lust or violence but on the more socially respectable (and therefore the more hidden and dangerous) sins. He scandalized His disciples with many hard sayings about detachment from worldly goods and about how hard it would be for a rich man to enter His kingdom.

James discovered the root of war in avarice when he wrote: "Where do wars and fights come from among you? Do they not come from your desires for pleasure that war in your members? You lust and do not have. You murder and covet and cannot obtain. You fight and war" (4:1–2). How many long and learned diagnoses of war and peace say as much as these two simple little verses?

Avarice has two parts: greed to get what we don't have and greed to keep what we have. Thus the two opposites of avarice are contentment, voluntary poverty, and liberality, generosity, having mercy on others.

Saint Paul says that "godliness with contentment is great gain," and "I have learned in whatever state I am to be content." Saint Francis courted Lady Poverty as a troubadour courted his lady fair. Sheldon Vanauken recounts, in *A Severe Mercy,* how he and his wife, Davy, dented their shiny new sports car with an axe. Saint Francis saw and approved, I think, as that was dissolving the glue on the flypaper.

As for liberality, "God loves a cheerful giver," and "It is more blessed to give than to receive." In a capitalist society we tend to think of giving as a means to receiving, even giving to God. Some evangelists ask for "seed money," appealing to avarice. They turn a gift into a spiritual investment. But Plato and Aristotle as well as Jesus taught that getting is a means of giving, that the best thing about getting riches is that this enables one to practice the virtue of magnanimity by giving it away.

Avarice is a special danger for our society for a number of reasons. First, our mobile society encourages competition and economic aggression rather than contentment. Someone who isn't climbing the social ladder is regarded as a fool and a failure. We're taught to climb to the top of the heap. What we're not taught is that the heap is a garbage heap. Compare Saint Paul's even more shocking four letter word for all his worldly possessions and privileges (see Phil.3:4–8 KJV).

Second, we are bombarded with advertising appeals to greed and media exaltations of affluence, from quiz shows to soaps. I think Jesus would consider "The Price is Right" more pornographic than *Deep Throat.*

Third, our whole capitalist economic system is based on the idea, taught by Adam Smith and John Locke, that a private evil can create a public good; that avarice (the profit motive) creates wealth and thereby happiness. From this point of view, our society's supposed opposite and great enemy, communism, is only a different means to the same end. Its means are totalitarian, not free; but its end, like ours, is the production and consumption of wealth, of things.

Fourth, an economic system based on money rather than on natural wealth (land, food, houses) has no natural, built-in limit to the flames of avarice. Since the desire for artificial wealth (money) is infinite, the miser always wants more. However the desire for natural wealth is only finite, as you can use only so much food and so many houses, unless you treat them as "investments," that is, as artificial wealth.

On a deeper level than the economic, avarice is a great unwisdom, a philosophical foolishness, for it assumes that happiness comes from possessing, from having things. That is a lie. Happiness can come only from being, not having. Happiness is in the heart, the center of one's being, and "the heart of man cannot hoard," according to George MacDonald. Only the hand can hoard.

Furthermore, we can possess only what is less than ourselves, things, objects. However we are possessed by what is greater than ourselves—God and His attributes, Truth, Goodness, Beauty. This alone can make one happy, can satisfy the restless heart, can fill the infinite, God-shaped hole at the center of one's being. Avarice simply doesn't work. It's like trying to fill the Grand Canyon with marbles.

The first skeleton archeologists uncovered from the volcanic ruins of ancient Pompeii was grasping silver coins in its outstretched skeletal hand. The coins rolled away as the skeleton was uncovered, with a mocking clink. Alexander the Great was a little wiser. After conquering the world and despairingly complaining that there were no more worlds to conquer, he soon died; but he directed that his bare hand would hang out of his coffin, to show the world that you can't take it with you. The wisdom of Job is literally true: "Naked I came into this world and naked I shall return."

If we are honest with ourselves and our experience, we soon learn that truth. Avarice defeats itself. Its very success proves its failure. Wealth soon palls and bores. No one is as bored as the rich who can echo Ecclesiastes, "I have seen everything." The cow of this world is milked dry.

Avarice is "the root of all evils" but it is "not the most grievous of sins," according to Saint Thomas. The pride that refuses to learn from repeated mistakes is that. The unpardonable sin is not any one sin but "final impenitence," the refusal to repent and receive God's total and freely offered forgiveness in Christ.

"Blessed are the merciful, for they shall obtain mercy."

The alternative to greed for getting is mercy in giving. Greed is less than justice, mercy is more. Mercy is a great mystery. The familiarity of the word blinds us to this fact. Mercy goes beyond reason (how could a computer understand it?), beyond justice, beyond right, beyond law. Where justice says "punish," mercy says "forgive." Where justice says "this is a debt," mercy says not that there is no debt but to dismiss the debt. To say there is no debt would be a lie since justice speaks the truth, and even mercy cannot contradict the truth, but mercy can say, "Dismiss the debt." *Dimitte debita nostra sicut et nos dimittimus debitoribus nostris* ("Dismiss to us our debts just as we dismiss those of our debtors").

A frequent mistake about mercy, one which hides its mystery, is to believe that it is a mere subjective attitude. That kind of mercy is not terribly costly. To change one's mind from seeking revenge to seeking the enemy's good is to give up only a moral headache. But real mercy is more, more mysterious, more objective, and more costly than that. It forgives debts that are objectively real, not subjectively imagined, debts that must be paid.

Mercy goes beyond justice, but does not undercut it. If I forgive you the one hundred dollar debt you owe me, that means I must use one hundred dollars more of my own money to pay my creditors. I cannot make you really one hundred dollars richer without making myself one hundred dollars poorer. If the debt is objectively real, it must be paid; and if it is my mercy that dismisses your debt, I must pay it. That is the reason why Christ had to die, why God could not simply say, "Forget it." He said, instead, "Forgive it." And that meant that if we did not pay it, He had to Himself.

Thus mercy is costly. Look what it cost God: the life of His infinitely dear Son.

And that is no exception, no freak, but the paradigm of mercy; thus we can expect mercy to cost us something, too.

That is the reason why it is paradoxical and surprising, why it is part of the good news, to hear Christ say that the merciful are blessed. We have come to expect paradox in the Beatitudes. Paradox is surprise, but it is not nonsense; it is apparent contradiction, but not real contradiction. So let us explore this paradox and find how this apparently unblessed, costly thing called mercy is really blessed.

It is blessed in four ways: in this life it is blessed from God; in this life from men; in the next life from God; and in the next life from men.

It is blessed from God in this life because God is the Master of the script of this life as well as the next. "He's got the whole world in His hands," and when we extend mercy, our self-sacrifice is always more than compensated for by God's grace to the giver. It is part of God's script that "it is more blessed to give than to receive." In addition to God's grace directly to the soul, there is usually abundant compensation to the mercy-giver through circumstances; for God is the Master of these too and arranges them to our good, sooner or later, if we only align ourselves with His will, His way, His plan. That plan *is* mercy because He is mercy.

Thus all who are merciful to others in this life are blessed by receiving mercy from God in this life. If we forgive, we are forgiven; if we forgive our fellows their small debts to us, God forgives us our great debts to Him. Love covers a multitude of sins.

Mercy is also blessed from humans in this life, simply because mercy is winsome. Even "the children of this world" know that, as Christ reminds us in the parable of the unjust steward (Luke 16:1–13), who made friends by means of his money by dismissing the debts of his master's creditors and thus obtained their mercy after his master fired him. His master commended him for his prudence. For we get what we give, in personal relationships as well as in economics. Bread cast on the waters, investments in mercy or in money, usually bears fruit. There are spiritual capital gains too. Everyone loves a lover, and people are merciful to the merciful. Nobody likes Scrooge!

Mercy is also blessed by God in the next life. Most of the rewards Christ promises in the Beatitudes have a double application, both to this life and to the next. It is not that God rewards the merciful in Heaven to compensate for their not being rewarded on earth, but that the heavenly rewards are the capstone, the completion, of the real but incomplete rewards in this life. They are not only the completion, but the natural and intrinsic completion as well. God's heavenly rewards for our earthly mercy are natural and necessary, not artificially added on. For our habit of being merciful is what makes us the kind of creatures that can accept and profit from God's mercy to ourselves.

Suppose God tried to reward an unmerciful man with mercy. It simply couldn't be done, not because God would withhold the gift, but because the hardened human heart would not receive it. Only those who are open to give mercy are open to receive it, and vice versa. Those who cannot give, cannot believe others can give and they distrust all gifts. We all know the type of person C. S. Lewis pictures in *The Great Divorce,* who says, "I stand on my rights, see? I don't want anybody's bleeding charity!" Since he has given no mercy, he expects and accepts none. But the only way to Heaven is to accept God's "bleeding charity" on Calvary.

Thus we reach the conclusion that strikes some with a silent, solemn shock, that there is simply no way to avoid Hell except by giving our fellow human beings mercy. Our Lord has commanded us to pray, "Forgive us our debts *as we forgive our debtors,*" so that if we do not forgive our debtors, we will be praying to God, "Do not forgive me, send me to Hell." We simply *cannot* pray the prayer all Christians must pray without being merciful. How clever and how merciful of Christ to include that impossibility in His prayer!

Finally, we receive mercy also from our fellows in the next life. This seldom-preached and seldom-realized truth is clearly taught in Christ's parable of the unjust steward: "And I say to you, make friends for yourselves by unrighteous mammon, that when you fail, they may receive you into everlasting habitations." Do we think our friends will be less able to demonstrate to us their gratitude for our earthly mercy to them in the next life than in this one?

God habitually uses secondary causes, especially human ones, to do His work. That is the work of the church. The Heavenly King has a great court; He spreads His grace and His work widely. In Heaven as on earth we receive God's grace through humanity. The archetype is Christ, of course. Through His humanity we are made partakers of divinity. This principle is not just temporary and earthly but in the very nature of things, and therefore perfected in Heaven.

Mercy is also one of the most practical things in the world. It is the only place to begin in trying to solve the problem of evil, the problem of sin. All humanity, sinners and saints alike, unbelievers and believers alike, Christians, Jews, Moslems, Hindus, Buddhists, animists, atheists, and agnostics can and must decide to live by mercy, or die. Unless we forgive, we fight; and when in our time the world has stockpiled enough weaponry to destroy every person on the planet many times over, mercy suddenly becomes infinitely practical. Forgiveness is the first step to solving the problem of war, wars between nations, families, and individuals. Even little children know this, perhaps little children best of all. They are not immune from sin; they, too, burn with hate and lust for vengeance, but they also are quick to forgive.

In a sense, strange as it sounds, we must even learn to forgive God, not for any evil, or debt He owes us, but for His very goodness. Why? He created us with that dangerous thing called free will which bowed to sin and brought its necessary punishments into the world, thus allowing us to suffer. He loves us far more than we would like, more than we find comfortable. We must forgive Him for interfering with our fond and foolish will again and again, forgive Him for His blessed but painful surgery on our spirits.

I think everyone has a secret resentment against God, against our very creation, against the fact of our being what we are. Freud called this the death-wish, resentment against being born into this pain-full world. The statue needs to forgive the sculptor for his love that causes the chisel's many blows to fall.

We need to stop complaining about bad things happening to good people, about injustice. There *are* no "good people," and the best of us say so the most clearly. Saints agree they are sinners; only sinners think they are saints. Only fools demand justice; for where would we be if we got it? No, mercy is our only hope from God, and our neighbors' only hope from us as well.

The convicted murderer deserves to die. Any consideration of capital punishment that does not begin there, with justice and the objective moral law and the rightness of punishment that fits the crime, any philosophy that refuses the truth in "an eye for an eye and a tooth for a tooth," is sentimentalism. Anyone who sees less than justice cannot see more. Justice is the precondition for mercy.

But once justice is admitted, we are free to be merciful. Once we get beyond the silly "there's nothing to forgive," we can forgive. Once we admit the justice of capital punishment or of defensive war, we can move ahead to seek better alternatives. But if justice and mercy are confused and we demand mercy as our just right, we understand (and probably receive) neither justice nor mercy.

Yet, though justice and mercy must be distinguished, there is a deep justice in transcending justice to mercy. That "the merciful . . . shall obtain mercy" is justice. Those who in virtue *go* beyond justice to mercy, *get* something beyond justice, mercy. And that is supremely just.

This illustrates the principle of transcendence: you must go beyond a thing to perfect it. The soul, not the body, perfects the body; God, not humanity, perfects humanity; mercy, not justice, perfects justice. We are constantly driven "upwards to the centre," in George MacDonald's phrase. We cannot fulfill the law of justice except by going beyond it to mercy, forgiveness, charity. Only "love is the fulfillment of the law." Only if we love our neighbor will we fulfill the demands of justice to that neighbor.

But even love drives us further "upwards towards the centre." For we cannot love merely by loving. As justice drives us to love, love drives us to union. Only in union with Love Himself can we love.

We love ourselves by nature. Only union between self and other enables us to love the other. God in His mercy has united us with Himself in Christ and with our fellows in Christ's Body, thereby enabling us to love Him and our neighbors as ourselves, for our neighbors have become one with ourselves in the single body, the family, the "New Man" that is the complete Christ, Head and Body.

The demand for mercy is God's *koan,* God's unsolvable puzzle to us, unsolvable in its own terms. "You shall be holy, for I the LORD your God am holy." Be righteous as I am with pure love, mercy beyond justice, self-forgetfulness. What a puzzle! How can a self be self-forgetful? Only by grace. How can we obey the law of justice? Only by love. How can we love? Only by grace. God's demands of justice and then of mercy and love drive us to the only possible solution: to Christ Himself.

CHAPTER NINE

Blessed Mourner vs. Mourning at Others' Blessedness (Envy)

ENVY

Saint Thomas defines envy as "sorrow at another's good." Envy is not the same as ambition or aspiration to have or attain the good that another person has. Such aspiration can be good, whether the good aspired to be a spiritual good (relation to God), a psychological good (relation to self or others), or even a material good (relation to things in the world), though the latter easily slides into avarice.

It is not envy to look up to another person. It is sanity and humility. Indeed, a world in which we never looked up to our superiors, a world in which "your betters" was forbidden language, a world without superiority, without hierarchy, and therefore without heroism, would be a deadly, dull, depressing, and despairing world. (Did I say "would be"?)

The good things of which envy is the counterfeit (for all evil counterfeits a good; Hell has very limited imagination) are rare and valuable: aspiration and heroism. Ernst Becker's Pulitzer-Prize-winning book *The Denial of Death* brilliantly demonstrated the truth of Nietzsche's theme that the modern world is becoming incapable of greatness or heroism.

A few years ago our teen-aged babysitter did the same, in her own way. She asked me to help her complete her project for English class. I was to talk spontaneously into her tape recorder for a minute about who my heroes were, so I uttered some obvious remarks about Jesus, Socrates, and my father, and she thanked me so profusely that I protested: "Just because I teach philosophy in college, that doesn't mean I have something better to say than someone else."

"Oh, but you did."

"But I only said the obvious."

"Maybe so, but it was different."

"How?"

"Everyone else I interviewed said something like: 'Heroes? What heroes? This is the twentieth century.'"

I was the only one who had any heroes. At first I felt sheepish; but after thinking about it, I felt grateful.

Aspiration looks up and says, "I aspire to be up there too." Saint Paul told Timothy that it is good to aspire to the office of bishop. Envy, on the other hand, looks up and says, "I want you to be below me." Envy is essentially competitive.

Why is envy a capital sin? What makes it so very bad?

Each of the seven deadly sins is in a different way the worst one. Envy, though not the greatest sin, is the only one that gives the sinner no pleasure at all, not even fake and temporary satisfaction. It causes nothing but pain and sorrow. Thus it shows more clearly than other sins the profound truths about the nature of all sin, that it removes our joy and that it is deceptive. The devil, who whispers his seductive advertisements into our ears, is a liar. His road leads to pure misery, not to satisfaction, much less to the joy we are always, deep down, seeking.

Envy removes joy because envy is the opposite of gratitude, and gratitude is the seedbed of joy. A man without gratitude is an ex-man, a protodemon. Every moment of our lives is an invitation to humanity, that is, to gratitude. We are always confronted by the half-full, half-empty glass. Our lives and our worlds are finite, never fully filled, never fully empty, so we always have opportunities for gratitude for the half full or ingratitude, resentment, and bitterness at the half empty and envy of those whose glass if fuller.

Another reason envy is a deadly sin is that it, like all the capital sins, leads to further sin—in this case to the worst sin of all: hatred, lovelessness. Anger leads to hatred too, but envy's road is shorter and more direct. For anger leads to hatred by way of gradual increase, by a disproportionate amount, when we want our enemies punished more than justice demands. However envy leads immediately to hatred, for envy is sorrow at another's good. Envy hates the other for having something good.

Envy is often the path that leads from pride, the greatest sin, to hatred, the lowest state of sin. As Saint Gregory the Great says in *Moralia* (XXXI, 45), "The spiritual vices are so clearly akin to one another that one springs from the others." Like cancer.

Envy is deadly because it is demonic. The ancient *Book of Wisdom* says, "By the envy of the devil, death came into the world." Pride and envy are Satan's own special sins. Envy is horrible because it comes straight from Hell.

Finally, envy is a deadly sin because it refuses our fundamental human situation of solidarity, neighborliness, family. The deepest and most important horizontal fact about our being is that we are our brother's keeper, and this is the reason for the second great commandment, to love our neighbor as ourselves. (The great vertical fact about our being is that we are creatures of God and beloved by God. That is the reason for the first commandment, to love God with our whole heart, soul, mind, and strength.)

We are commanded to "rejoice with those who rejoice, and weep with those who weep." As Gabriel Marcel puts it, our very mode of being is a "with-being" *(co-esse)*. Envy is not *with* but *at*. It weeps at those who rejoice and rejoices at those who weep. It refuses the primal fact of the family, the Body, both secular and sacred, or Mystical. It enacts the falsehood of alienation instead of the truth of solidarity. That is the reason why it is a leading cause of war in our history and in our lives.

Saint Augustine expresses wonder at the discovery that although all material things diminish when shared, spiritual things do not; in fact, they increase. If I give you some of my money or food, I have that much less left for myself. But if I give you some love or knowledge, I do not diminish my share of them; I increase it. Envy proceeds from the myopic view of good as nonsharable. Its cure is the experience of sharable goods, especially love. ("Love covers a multitude of sins.")

This perennial source of envy is joined by a specifically modern one in our egalitarian age. Democracy, a wise and practical idea in politics, becomes foolish and unrealistic when extended to our spiritual lives. God's government is theocracy, not democracy. When we think that because we are made equal in political rights by our society, we are in fact equal spiritually, it is simply not true. Scripture is violated. Judas is not the spiritual equal to John, or even Lot to Abraham.

But is it not before God that we are all equal? If so, why does He separate sheep from goats?

Are not all the sheep equal? If so, why does Saint Paul describe the resurrection by saying that "star differs from star in glory"? And why does our Lord consistently tell parables about unequal rewards, such as seed, talents, ruling cities?

If all this rankles, we are prone to envy in its modern form. Its word is, "I'm just as good as you." As C. S. Lewis points out, no one who ever said that believed it. It is the word of the one who feels inferior and resents it.

In a world in which people really are superior and inferior to each other in many ways, and in which an ideology of absolute egalitarianism forbids us to admit that fact, the jarring misfit between this ideology and reality expresses itself as resentful envy.

Radical feminists, for instance, seem to be prone to this envy when they demand "freedom" from their wombs and from their babies, resenting God or Nature's making them different from men and often doing all they can to imitate men, resenting what they are and envying what they are not. (Women really are superior to men—at being women. And men are really superior to women—at being men.)

There is another distinctively modern form of envy, which is collective rather than individual. It is our secular society's unconscious envy of Eden, of Paradise, of divine perfection. It is our attempt to sneak under the seraphim's flaming sword back into Eden by making a Heaven on earth, by rebuilding the Tower of Babel, by finding salvation and happiness in the City of the World rather than in the City of God.

Nietzsche revealed the psychological origin of this demand when he wrote, "A man can endure almost any *how* if only he has a *why*." He meant that we can endure very imperfect circumstances, even great suffering, if only we have a meaning, a purpose for it all. The corollary of this truth is that if we do *not* have a *why*, a deeply felt and lived purpose, that is, if we are typically modern, then we will not endure any *how*, any world that is even mildly upsetting. We will demand a degree of comfort, security, and control undreamed of by any other society. And we will find the technological and political means to create it even if it kills us. And it will.

God has pulled the teeth of envy by the Incarnation. There is no longer any reason to envy a God who is crowned with thorns and suffers the pains of Hell itself on the cross.

The opposite of envy is contentment even when mourning. We can be content with this Christ. Instead of sorrowing at another's good, we can rejoice at His sorrows, and at our own, for they are now part of His.

This sounds like an impossible paradox. How can we rejoice in sorrow? How can tears constitute a smile? We can understand this only if we distinguish *blessedness* from *happiness*. The next beatitude shows us how.

"Blessed are those who mourn, for they shall be comforted."

This beatitude is the direct refutation of the confusion between blessedness and happiness, and of the misleading translation, "Happy are those who mourn." Mourning is essentially an expression of *un*happiness, and Jesus did not utter empty contradictions like "Happy are those who are unhappy."

The world is the source of mourning. It is, and will be until the end of time, a vale of tears, despite our honest but doomed attempts to turn it into a Paradise, and also despite our dishonest but largely successful attempts to deny that basic truth to ourselves.

"In the world you will have tribulation," said the Lord to His disciples (and to us, unless we are no longer His disciples), "but be of good cheer, I have overcome the world" (John 16:33). The comfort Jesus promised to those who mourn is His, not the world's: "Not as the world gives, do I give to you" (John 14:27).

Who are the blessed who mourn?

Those who mourn are not only those who express sorrow openly by tears, but are all those who experience sorrow. Blessed are the sorrowful, blessed are the sufferers. This beatitude is about suffering, the thing we fear more than death itself. Christ tells us here the most startling thing we've ever heard about that which frightens us most. His words sway on the brink of nonsense, but they do not fall. Instead, they dance. He says, in effect, "The thing you fear most is a great blessing. You fear a great good more than you fear great evils."

Who are these mourners who are blessed? All people mourn, so all can be blessed in their mourning. But not all are blessed. The gift is offered to all, but not all receive it, for it does not look like a gift. Faith in appearances does not receive this gift; faith in God's words does. Every gift requires two freedoms: the giver's and the receiver's. This is as true of all the attendant blessings of salvation as it is of salvation itself; thus it is true of this beatitude, this blessing, too.

All can be blessed by mourning. But we can distinguish levels and degrees. First, ordinary human suffering is blessed, any suffering, from a headache to dying. Every suffering can be blessed because it hollows out a place in us for God and His comfort, which is infinite joy. Finite sorrows fertilize the soul's soil so that the plant of infinite joy can grow. Sorrows sensitize the soul both to sorrow and also to joy. The more we suffer, the more we appreciate joy. If this truism holds even of earthly joys, how infinitely more worthwhile to suffer the brief sorrows of this world so as to appreciate better the eternal and perfect joys of the next! Our sorrows, we are told, work an "eternal weight of glory" in us.

If even suffering for ourselves can be blessed, suffering for others can be doubly blessed. For this reproduces the pattern of Christ's suffering, the Vine patterning its branches, the Head patterning His Body. And the greatest possible suffering is blessed most of all. What is that? Any lover knows. Not only can the soul suffer far more than the body, but the center of the soul, the heart which loves, can suffer most of all.

Simply, the more you love the more you suffer. Infinite Love, therefore, is capable of infinite suffering. That's how one Man literally suffered all the sufferings of the whole human race. Infinity can include all finitudes. It was not His physical thorns or His physical thirst but the thorns of our rejection of His love and His thirst for lost souls that tortured Christ on the cross infinitely, and was infinitely blessed with the triumph of a lost race saved.

Why is it that nothing can make us as sorrowful as love? It is the same reason that nothing can make us as joyful as love. In love we become the other, we slough off our skin like a snake. Underneath that hard, protective coat of otherness and ego, there is new flesh, incomparably more sensitive than the outer skin. The heart is like a newborn baby. It is our spiritual erogenous zone, capable of exquisite joys *and* exquisite sufferings by its extreme sensitivity. We appropriately cover and protect these privy parts of the soul, just as we do to the corresponding parts of the body. But when we love, we expose them, to pleasures or pains beyond imagining.

That is why the Man of Sorrows is also the Man of Joy, "who for the joy that was set before Him endured the cross" (Heb. 12:2). The joy of the crown outweighs even the pain of the Cross. "For I consider that the sufferings of this present time are not worthy to be compared with the glory which shall be revealed in us" (Rom. 8:18).

In fact, not only is there anticipated joy, the joy in hope of Heaven as the child of earth's labor pains, but there is even joy here and now *in* (though not *because of*) the sufferings. "*In* all these things we are more than conquerors" (Rom. 8:37). The Church will not canonize a saint without proof of extraordinary joy in his life.

If suffering is blessed, suffering for others doubly blessed, and suffering for love triply blessed, then suffering for Christ is quadruply blessed. Not an option for supersaints, suffering for Christ is a universal requirement for all Christians. We are all required as a condition of our very salvation to die to our self-will and to grow into the pattern of Christ, who said he came "not to do My own will, but the will of Him who sent Me." To die to self-will and self-interest is to suffer. Old Adam screams in our ear, "Don't let that One get too close; He wants to kill me!" And Old Adam is right.

Some of us are called to endure special sufferings for Christ, persecutions, which will be the subject of the last Beatitude. All of us are required to be ready and willing to endure persecution for Christ; but even those who are not persecuted must suffer the death of self for Christ, or else Christ cannot be born in them. If Adam will not die in us, then Advent will have happened only once in the world, long ago, and not in our souls. God will come and miraculously pitch His tent in our souls only if the soul is like Mary, ready to say, "Let it be done to me according to your word."

A concrete example of suffering for Christ could be the mother who refuses to get an abortion at the price of great personal suffering, physically, socially, and emotionally. We who clearly see the horror of abortion often fail to see the lesser but real horror of alternatives, the sacrifice borne by an unmarried teenage girl, an older woman, or a victim of rape. However, virtue is willing to suffer.

Another example of suffering for Christ is obedience to the commandment against adultery, premarital or extramarital sex. In our present condition of unnatural consciousness in this unnatural society, such obedience often appears as heroic sacrifice rather than joy. Even so, if it is done out of love for Christ and commitment to Christian virtue, it is blessed. Indeed, the very unnaturalness that darkens our modern eyes to the joy and beauty of chastity and fidelity can work for blessing when it makes what was easy and natural for previous generations into a heroic and difficult sacrifice whose only reason becomes obedience to the Christ we love. This is not the ideal condition of consciousness, of course; but even the sufferings caused by this modern error can be used by God and blessed.

Finally, a quintuple blessing rests on voluntary spiritual discipline, sacrifices willingly undertaken out of love for Christ: the mortifications of the flesh so familiar in the lives of the saints and so utterly incomprehensible to the modern mind. That such voluntary disciplines are God's will for all Christians is proved by Scripture's calls to fast and to give alms.

Any sacrifice, however small, voluntarily offered up in faith and love is blessed. Ordinary physical sufferings that come to all of us, like illnesses, afford opportunity to offer it up. But temptations to personal resentment, revenge, greed, lust, pride, or anger can also be renounced and offered up to Christ with even greater blessing.

How does mourning (suffering) bless us? First it trains us by sculpting souls. This is God's work, not ours. The sculptor, not the statue, knows when and where the hammer must fall. Second, it strengthens our love, the motive for enduring suffering. After we invest a lot of suffering in something, we treasure it more, for "where your treasure is, there your heart will be also." Third, it teaches us the wisdom that comes only by the experience of suffering. Rabbi Abraham Heschel puts it simply: "The man who has not suffered—what can he know, anyway?"

What does suffering teach? The wordless wisdom that even sinners can detect in saints. The thing that made Job finally satisfied. Even Christ, "though He was a Son, yet He learned obedience by the things which He suffered" (Heb. 5:8).

"Mourning" connotes not just suffering but also death, our last enemy that Christ has made our greatest blessing: "Thou hast made death glorious and triumphant, for through its portals we enter into the presence of the living God," says the anthem.

The heart's horrible cry of mourning has been turned into the shout of victory, because the worst thing that ever happened, deicide, Satan's closing of his trap on God Himself there on the cross when God was forsaken of God, has become *Good* Friday, the best thing that ever happened, our salvation. The Beatitudes get their paradoxical power from that fact. And so do we.

CHAPTER TEN

The Meek and Peacemakers vs.
The Anger-driven

ANGER

Anger (*ira* in Latin, "wrath" in Old English) is one of the Seven Deadly Sins. But what most people mean by "anger" is often not a sin at all. What most people mean by "anger" is simply an emotion; and no emotion, merely as an emotion, is a sin, because we cannot directly control the arising of an emotion in our soul. Therefore, we are not directly responsible for it. Only when an element of the will is added is there any sin, including the sin of anger.

This can be done in a number of different ways. The will can command an emotion to rise, to flourish, or to cease. Often these commands will be weak and not obeyed by the emotions, which are often stronger than the will. But even so, whenever we will anything we are responsible for it.

The commonest way in which the will comes in to make an emotion sinful or virtuous is by consent, which is basically the will's approval, or go-ahead to an emotion. When the emotion ought to be opposed and is not, the will sins. For instance, if we know we ought not to be as angry as we are toward someone, yet we continue to will that anger, we sin.

What makes the emotion of anger into the sin of anger are two

129

things. First, as we have already seen, there must be the involve-
ment of the will. Second, the anger must be inordinate, that is,
wrong, irrational, too strong for the occasion or the person we are
angry at. Emotions can be rational or irrational just as thoughts
can; the modern prejudice to the contrary is quite irrational. Saint
John Chrysostom says, "He that is angry without cause shall be in
danger, but he that is angry with cause shall not" (*Homily* 10). In
other words, getting angry at the wrong things, or getting too
angry, is sinful; but getting rightfully angry, angry at the right
things and to an appropriate degree, is not. The Psalmist shows
this to be true when he writes, "Be angry, and sin not" (Ps. 4:4).

Chrysostom also says, "He who is not angry when he has cause
to be, sins. For unreasonable patience is the hotbed of many
vices." As a more contemporary source has it, "The only thing
necessary for the triumph of evil is for good men to do nothing." To
be angry at the lawyer who got the drug pusher free on a techni-
cality is not sinful, especially when your son is lying in a coffin
after an overdose from that pusher. *Not* to be angry in this case
would be more sinful than almost any conceivable anger. To be
angry at the religious huckster and hypocrite who uses God's
name to sucker naive young people, their money, their loyalty, and
perhaps their souls, into his power-hungry cult is not a sin. It is
holy. To be angry at a doctor who makes a fortune running an
abortion clinic and pressuring distraught mothers to let him kill
their unborn babies is not a sin. It is a crusade. To see a crippled
or retarded child and not to be angry at the doctor whose gross
negligence was responsible is not a sin. It is godlike.

For God Himself has anger ("wrath") according to His own
word. And to be like God is not sinful. Therefore anger is not by
itself sinful.

We know that God has "wrath" both from the Old Testament,

in which God's character (including His wrath) is revealed through the words of His inspired prophets, His mouthpieces; and from the New Testament, where His character is most fully revealed in the character and personality of Jesus, Whom Scripture calls "the image of the invisible God. . . . in Him all the fullness should dwell" (Col. 1:15, 19). And Jesus got angry. He got so angry at the moneychangers in the temple that he became God's bouncer and whipped their unholy business out of His own holy house, as a father would beat up a robber who was breaking and entering his own family's house. He repeatedly got angry at the Pharisees for binding heavy burdens on the poor and not lifting a finger to help bear them, and for their own icy arrogance and self-righteousness when face to face with God in the flesh.

So God has anger. What kind of anger? The wrath of God is a true, real, and proper description of something really in God; but is it the same kind of anger we find in ourselves, or is it only similar to it by way of analogy or symbol?

Nearly all great Christian theologians of the past agree that it is by way of analogy or symbol. "'For My thoughts are not your thoughts,/Nor are your ways My ways,' says the LORD./'For as the heavens are higher than the earth,/So are My ways higher than your ways,/And My thoughts than your thoughts'" (Isa. 55:8–9). This does not mean that the wrath of God is a mere approximation or pale copy of human anger; it means that human anger is a mere approximation or pale copy of divine wrath. It does not mean that the wrath of God is a primitive myth or a man-made fiction, like the boogieman or Santa Claus. Just as "the strong right arm of God" refers to real power in God, though not literally and physically of the power of a biological arm, so "the wrath of God" refers to something real, though not the intermittent, environmentally-stimulated, and often irrational thing we call "anger" in ourselves. For it is changeless; it flows from God's inner nature, not any external conditioning; and it is neither irrational nor a passion (*passio,* "passivity," "being influenced by another"). It is His justice, His perfect holiness, experienced as wrath by its (His) enemies, but as goodness by His friends.

This last point may be clarified by recalling a "shewing" God gave to the Lady Julian of Norwich. She asked God if she could please see His wrath, because she was disturbed at reading about it in Scripture (which she knew to be God's word and true), since she knew both from that same Scripture and from her own experience that God was pure love (*Revelations of Divine Love* XLVIII). So God showed her His wrath. And she said of this "shewing," "I saw no wrath but on Man's part."

What does this mean? I think it means something like this. God is all goodness, all love. He is not love plus justice, or goodness plus wrath. God's goodness and love reflect justice, holiness, moral goodness. God loves what is good, not what is evil. When we hate what is good and love what is evil, when we hate what God loves, and what God *is,* and love what God hates, then God Himself seems to us to be our enemy and to be angry with us.

In fact it is only our sin which He is angry at. But when we identify with that sin rather than dissociating ourselves from it by repentance, then it seems to us that it is ourselves, not just our sin, that God is angry at. However when we dissolve by the solvent of repentance the glue that glues us to our sins, then we know that God, in hating our sin, is like a surgeon who hates the cancer only because he loves the patient.

We are commanded to "love the sinner and hate the sin." This applies to ourselves as well as to our neighbors, for we are to love our neighbors *as ourselves.* Then how dare we think that God does not practice the same morality He preaches to us? Is God an Omnipotent Hypocrite? If not, two conclusions follow: God really is angry at sin, and God really loves sinners.

This sounds familiar and pretty safe, but it has implications that would upset many people. First, since God is really angry at sin, our modern morality of niceness, togetherness, and tolerance is far from God's morality. God is no more an omnipotent Chum than He is an omnipotent Fiend. Second, since God really loves sinners, our tendency to let anger settle into a simmering hate is even farther from God's mind. If Adolf Hitler had come to Jesus truly repentant, Jesus would have forgiven him, even if that act would have scandalized millions of Jewish mothers whose sons had died in concentration camps. Jesus forgave Mary Magdalene. Do you think there were no wives whose marriages had been destroyed by her and felt resentment at His forgiveness? If they did, it is because they failed to do that thing that is so easy to say and so hard to do: hate the sin and love the sinner.

The worst thing about anger is that it tends to lead to hatred. Anger becomes a mortal sin, says Aquinas, "if through the fierceness of his anger a man fall away from the love of God and his neighbor." Anger is not always contrary to love; we usually get angriest at those we love the most. But when anger becomes settled hatred, it is mortal sin. When anger's heat turns to rigid coldness, it is rigor mortis.

The reason that anger is called a capital sin is just this, not just for what it is in itself but for what it leads to, for all the capital sins are seeds for further sin. *Capital* comes from *caput*, "head"; as the head leads the rest of the body, so the capital sins lead the rest of the sins. And anger's special danger is that it leads to the worst sin of all, hatred, the opposite of love, which is the greatest good. This is why hatred is not one of the seven capital sins, as Saint Thomas explains: it is not the source of further sins because it is as bad as you can get; it is the last stage of sin, the satanic stage. Satan is pure hatred, as God is pure love.

This is the reason why it is crucial to distinguish anger from hatred. There is a kind of anger (the nonsinful kind) which, as we have seen, is in God Himself, while hate is not in God but is in Satan. If we do not clearly distinguish anger from hatred, then we do not clearly distinguish God from Satan!

The difference is that hatred wills evil to its object, while anger sometimes wills good. Hatred's completest expression is "Damn you!" (In our secularized and unbelieving culture, fortunately, this is seldom meant literally.) But anger sometimes is a will to good: the good of deserved and needed punishment, the will to justice and correction.

We can, then, distinguish four levels of anger. First, there is simply the emotion itself. This is neither good nor evil, though it may be a psychological difficulty, a problem of temper. Second, there is this emotion rightly regulated by reason, the will to justice and correction. Third, there is the emotion overstepping the bounds of right reason, and this is the capital sin of anger. Saint Thomas defines this as the desire that another person be punished "who has not deserved it, or beyond his deserts, or contrary to the order prescribed by law, or not for the due end, namely the maintaining of justice and the correction of fault." Finally, there is the stage where anger turns to hatred of God or neighbor.

Because of this mortal danger, meekness, gentleness, and patience are such practically useful virtues. They steer us away from the cliff.

There are *two* beatitudes that confront the deadly sin of anger: meekness and its characteristic work, peacemaking. We explore them now in turn.

> "Blessed are the meek,
> for they shall inherit the earth."

All the sources and commentaries I could find on this verse had two things in common: they wanted to distinguish clearly what Jesus meant by the meek from what the world means (and scorns); and though they wanted to, they couldn't. The execution did not match the intention. I got the impression (and I think many other readers do too) that here is a weak point, a sore spot, that the supposed difference between meekness and weakness is only a verbal cover-up.

Therefore let one more commentator rush in where angelic ones have not feared to tread. What did Jesus *not* mean by "the meek"? What *did* he mean? And how will they inherit the earth?

First, the meek are not the weak. The rhyme unconsciously suggests the connection. So let us counter it by something else from the unconscious, an image rather than a definition. Think of the ideal medieval knight. The true knight combines without compromise great strength and great meekness, the ability to use force and the gentleness to forego it, the willingness to brave perilous quests and the gentle courtesy of a Platonic lover. He is a man, but a gentle-man.

Also think of the character traits of a Nietzsche or a Hitler sanctified. Suppose God had arranged for these two virulent anti-Christs to have become saints! Meekness is present in all the saints, even in Augustine, in Jerome, in Ignatius Loyola. Saints Friedrich and Adolf would have been modern Saint Pauls. What a waste of *spirit* they were!

We rightly think of the meek as the opposite of the bully. But the bully has two opposites, not one: the meek and the weak. The weak in spirit, the timid and cowardly and fearful, are not as complete an opposite to the bully as are the meek, for a coward is a potential bully. One of the most common motivations for bullying is the feeling of weakness and inferiority. On a deeper level, a person who sees himself as metaphysically weak, as ghostlike in his being, may want to assure himself of his substance, his reality, of the fact that he is alive, by the two most desperate acts of bullying: rape and murder, entering the living body of another forcibly to create or destroy life. Indeed, modern people are generally speaking in this ghostlike condition, and that is the reason why they are vicariously fascinated with rape and murder, as media writers well know and exploit.

But the world will not be convinced that meekness is not weakness until it sees what meekness *is*. Understanding it by contrast with its opposite is necessary but not sufficient.

To see what meekness is, you must look not at meekness but at Christ. Saying meekness is this or that sends you to concepts which are pale copies of reality. Saying "Jesus is meek" sends you to the living reality of it. Well, what of His meekness?

One thing Jesus certainly is not is tame. "Aslan is not a tame lion," as they say in Narnia. The Lion of the tribe of Judah is feared, so feared that He is crucified. He never simpers and often roars. His very language shows a penchant for giantesque metaphor: millstones around the neck, whitened sepulchres, logs in the eyes, gnashing of hellish teeth. No one in Scripture ever talked more about Hell than Jesus did, by the way.

But all Jesus' roaring, including His hell-fire and damnation sermons to the Pharisees, was to help rather than to harm. When shock therapy was needed, Jesus did not offer sweetness and light. He was always "the man for others," ready to suffer harm rather than to cause it, in fact ready to suffer harm in order to uncause it, to undo it. The essence of meekness is this: not to cause harm.

But we cause harm by omission as well as by commission.

Meekness, therefore, is not sitting on the sidelines when action is needed. Meekness is that aspect of selflessness which avoids harming, whether by action or inaction. It takes a big self to be selfless. A small self desperately holds itself together and is "into" itself.

Meekness is, therefore, a kind of submissiveness, but not to the environment, to circumstances, to whatever happens to be strong out there. It is submissiveness to God, not to the world. This is the reason why meekness is dynamic, because God is dynamic. Aggressive worldliness is not dynamic, for the world is far less dynamic than God. Once you've made your million, or become president of the company, the dynamism peaks and fails, like the coming of old age; but "those who wait on the LORD/Shall renew their strength;/They shall mount up with wings like eagles;/They shall run and not be weary,/They shall walk and not be faint" (Isa. 40:31).

And the motive for the submissiveness of meekness is not weakness, fear, or laziness, but the energy and confidence and idealism of love. Submitting to a tyrant is exactly the opposite of submitting to a lover. The first takes a diminution of spiritual energy, the second takes an excess.

We fail to see the energy in submissiveness because there is an automatic cry of "male chauvinism" from the world in its prejudice against submissiveness. Women have nearly always been regarded as the weaker sex. However, even physically this is true only in certain situations. Men play football better, but women live longer and bear babies better! The physical fact that a woman is on the receiving end in intercourse, coupled with the fact that the physical is the image of the spiritual (unless we are ghosts in machines rather than psychosomatic unities), leads logically to the conclusion that a woman's spirit, like her body, is by nature more submissive than a man's. The male chauvinist agrees with this conclusion but sees it as proof of a woman's inferiority. The modern unisexist or antisexist disagrees with the conclusion because it seems to lead to the chauvinist corollary. But both feminists and "male-ists" misunderstand submissiveness. Submissiveness is not weakness or inferiority.

Jesus was submissive, utterly submissive to His Father. "I come not to do my own will, but the will of Him who sent Me." Jesus is the definitive, revolutionary refutation of male chauvinism without the foolishness of unisexism. He revolutionizes submissiveness; He shows it as a mark of strength, not weakness. He is submissive to His Father while being absolutely equal to Him, sharing fully and completely the divine nature. Jesus Christ forever shows us what it means for sons to submit to fathers, wives to husbands, the Church to God Himself. "Spiritually, we are all feminine," say the mystics. And that is one secret of our strength!

This is the reason why Scripture attaches such tremendous promises to the meek and submissive spirit. Strength is an inevitable and natural consequence of submissiveness to God. What goes in the submissive end of the tube comes out the active end: God's own life. Once you let God into you, you have God in you. And God is a dynamo.

It is not that God, to compensate for the injustice done to the meek because of their meekness, miraculously grants them blessings from above, in contradiction to their natural deprivations from below. Rather, the inherent nature of meekness naturally taps in to these blessings, as woman to man, earth to sun, ground to water, mouth to food, electricity to dynamo. Thus "the meek shall eat and be satisfied"; "he will guide the meek in judgment"; "the Lord lifteth up all the meek"; "he will beautify the meek with salvation"; "the meek shall increase their joy in the Lord"; and, above all, there is Mary's Magnificat, a paean of paradox to praise the magnificence of meekness, the hymn of happiness of holy humility.

Meekness is an aspect of humility, the first and prerequisite virtue, the alternative to the first and deadliest sin, pride. Meekness is what Christ is, both in Heaven and on earth. In Heaven, from before all time, He has been eternally obedient to His father in joy, and He graciously reveals to us in the Beatitudes the nature of this relationship so that we too can share that joy, which is the very life of God. And on earth, too, the God-man says, "I am meek and humble of heart." This is the man who turned the world upside down, the man the world had either to crucify or worship.

How, then, do the meek inherit the earth? The meek do not inherit this world and its ruling powers, for it will pass away. Jesus was not enthroned by the world but crucified, and He is not our exception but our paradigm. No, inheritance presupposes death. Children inherit parents' fortunes when they die. This earth, Mother Earth, like a parent, has its fortunes in God's storage bank, for God is the creator of the earth, after all, and is its rightful owner; "the cattle on a thousand hills" are His. After this present order dies, we will inherit the new earth promised in Revelation.

When we (Adam) fell, our earth fell with us, for we were its custodian and priest. In fact the earth is like our extended body. Therefore the resurrection body includes "the new heavens and the new earth" as its own new extended body. We inherit the new earth through death and resurrection. Meekness submits even to death, because beyond its dark door lies the light of new life.

Meanwhile, what of Monday morning? Meekness is not only an investment for eternity, it is also the most practical of necessities here and now. There is a startlingly literal sense in which this beatitude comes alive in our century. The meek, those who do no harm, will *have* an earth to inherit, while those who assert themselves and their power against others will have neither power nor self nor earth to inherit.

Ecologically, we can ruin or repair, sack or save, loot or love our

Mother Earth. But even more crucially, we can through lack of meekness destroy our entire planet's life and our own in a fit of childish pique, unleashing hellfire on this world, a universal Sodom and Gomorrah, with our nuclear toys. Only the meek will have an earth to inherit, in this life as well as in the life to come. The Beatitudes nowhere show their practical and universal truth better than here. They are not pious ideals for supersaints, but the sane, the only, the absolutely necessary plan for survival for the whole world. Unless we practice meekness, we will all die.

The woman who pays a physician to slaughter her unborn son or daughter because she wants to decide who shall live and who shall die—is she meek? The man who encourages, prods, or consents to her doing this—is he meek? The theologian or philosopher who arrogates to mankind the right to decide under what conditions human life is "meaningful" enough and of a sufficiently high "quality" to escape euthanasia—is he meek? The leader who orders a nuclear strike—is he meek?

George Bernard Shaw proposed in the play "On the Rocks" that in the Utopia of the future each citizen would have to prove to a central committee that his life was socially useful, or else he would be disposed of painlessly and efficiently. If Hitler had not shown us the results of just such a "quality of life" ethic in the most graphic possible way, the "advanced" nations of our world would almost certainly be practicing something very similar today. The same extermination policies of Hitler's Germany, the very first nation in history to legalize euthanasia, is suddenly being reconsidered again by Western nations.

The world is at a turning point. With the new powers, nuclear, genetic, and psychological, that are around our corner, we are becoming more and more like gods. In all our history, only one Man could be a god and still be meek. We must return to the virtue which is His. Only His way can save our world. Meekness is the only road to peace.

> **"Blessed are the peacemakers,
> for they shall be called sons of God."**

Only once before in our history was it so crucial to know what peace is and how to make it. Only once before in our history was civilization itself in danger. Rome *was* civilization, and Rome fell. Saint Augustine lived through this trauma, the trauma of our past that most resembled the possible nuclear trauma of our future; and his response to it was to write one of the greatest and most important books ever written, *The City of God,* the world's first philosophy of history. This book is about peace, for Augustine identifies the end of a city, or society, as peace.

Peace is an absolute necessity again in our age. Those who are not utterly appalled by the prospect of nuclear war are like those who are not utterly appalled by the prospect of abortion: they don't *look*. If we look at the truth, at the data, if we look at the real possibility of three billion corpses, if we look at the present actuality of millions of dismembered, scalded human babies, then no argument about the morality of these things is needed.

The next global war would not be our first, but it would quite possibly be our last. At no time in history has peace been so crucial a prize, not just to think about but to achieve, not just to understand but to create.

But we cannot create it if we do not understand it. We cannot achieve it if we do not think about it. We cannot be peacemakers unless we know what peace is. Thus two questions are crucial to our age: what peace is and how to make it.

Peace, says Augustine, is not merely the absence of war. Peace is positive. It is rest in our end. After the stone falls, it is at peace. After the acorn grows into the oak tree, it is at peace in its treehood and does not grow any further. After the animal's hunger is sated with food, it is at peace. And the human heart? Because "Thou hast made us for Thyself," therefore "our hearts are restless until they rest in Thee." For man, *peace* is another word for God.

Peace in "the City of the World" is external, military, political; and the members of "the City of God" should cooperate in this end. But this peace is flower, not root. Only "the City of God" has peace at its root, at its heart. Thomas Merton said simply in *Seeds of Contemplation:* "We are not at peace with others because we are not at peace with ourselves, and we are not at peace with ourselves because we are not at peace with God." That is the best diagnosis I have ever read. Now what of the cure?

Trace the word *peace* through the Scriptures with a concordance, and one of the first and most unavoidable things you learn is that God is its sole Author. That is the reason why Jesus calls peacemakers "sons of God," for like Father, like son.

A son of God does more than believe in peace, hope for peace, and love peace, though these three things are a necessary beginning. The beatitude does not say merely: "Blessed are the peacelovers," but something rarer, "Blessed are the peace-makers," those who effect the peace that is loved.

Nearly everyone wants peace. All sane persons prefer peace to war. The aim and end of war is peace, not vice versa. But not many know the way to make peace. The beatitude is terribly practical; it gives us what we need: the way to peace.

What, then, is the way? How can we make peace?

Christ is the Way. The way to make peace is by becoming a Christ, by becoming a different person, by getting a new nature by a new birth. *Operatio sequitur esse* ("action follows being"), says the wise medieval cliché. You *make* peace by *being* a peacemaker. And that means being a son of God. Only God and His children can make peace. That's why peacemakers "shall be called the sons of God," known as the sons of God. Their work is a sign and effect of their being.

It's not that peacemaking makes you a child of God, but that being a child of God makes you a peacemaker. Jesus does not say, "Blessed are the peacemakers, for they shall *become* the sons of God," but "they shall be *called* (known as) the sons of God." The cause is known from its effects.

A son of God, of course, means being much more than an imitator of God, more even than being a lover of God. It means being a sharer in the divine nature, being a human garden which has allowed God to plant the seed of His own life in it. And that means Christ, "God become man that man may become God." Once again the beatitude points us to Christ. Christ does not merely give us the Beatitudes; the Beatitudes lead us to Christ. They are puzzles to which Christ alone is the answer, for peacemaking is a divine-human work, and only the Divine-Human One can do it.

But wait. Let's not let piety substitute for questioning. Here is an honest question: Haven't many unbelievers made peace?

Here is the honest answer, unacceptable as it will be to the world: No, not lasting peace, rooted peace, real peace, permanent peace. Our poor world's history is a history of war, not a history of peace. It is a history of a few oases of peace surrounded by an immense desert of war, not a history of an immense sea of peace troubled by occasional storms of war. Man without God has not in fact been able to make even external peace.

But what about *men* with God? Isn't it also true that Christians have often chosen war rather than peace as a way of solving problems? Alas, yes, some of the bloodiest wars in history were religious wars, such as the Crusades, the Thirty Years' War, the

Spanish Inquisition. Just as you and I as children have often willfully disobeyed our parents, so we as the children of God have turned from our Father in Heaven and from the Prince of Peace. But insofar as we did this, we were not "man with God" but "man against God." Man without God—unbelievers—has not made peace. Man against God—God's own children turning away from Him—has not made peace. Only man *with* God has made peace, and the only Man who was totally one with God is Christ.

Christ made peace. His methods were not military or even political, though many expected the Messiah to be a new Saul, David, or Solomon. Similarly, many today expect the gospel to be identified with some social gospel or some political system, with the Left or the Right, with some liberation from social structures of the opposite stripe, which is confused with liberation from sin. It is the same kind of confusion Jesus' disciples continually made when they expected Jesus to fit into their expectations and their categories.

How did Christ make peace? He whipped the moneychangers, as a father would whip a thief who entered his house, for it *was* His Father's house. But He did not allow His disciples to use the sword as a policy, publicly, even to defend the most worthy cause and the most innocent Person who ever existed. In the Garden of Gethsemane, He commanded Peter to put up his sword and reminded him that those who live by the sword perish by the sword. Thus the most just war ever fought, in defense of the most just, most worthy, most innocent Man and cause, was also the shortest. Jesus stopped it almost before it started, apparently allowing it to start only to give His disciples and us an object lesson about His methods for ending it. After stopping the war, he healed its lone casualty, Malchus, whose ear had been cut off. Then, having made peace in this local and physical war, He went on to make peace in the universal, spiritual war, the war between man and God, on Calvary.

There too He did not use force but made peace in the most surprising way, by dying. He drained away war down Himself, like a sinkhole, or a blotter. He made peace by making Himself the universal victim, by suffering all the violence, war, aggression, hate, and harm that the father of lies and of violence could fling at Him, by doing nothing in return, by being meek as the slaughtered sheep. *He* was "the meek" who "shall inherit the earth." By His meekness He won the world and the authority to give its rule over to His disciples when the time is ripe.

A strange story indeed, the strangest story ever told. It is symbolized in Revelation by the battle between *therion,* the Great Beast, and *arnion,* the meek little Lamb; and the odds are stacked, for the Beast doesn't stand a chance against the strategy of the Lamb, who wins by losing, triumphs by dying.

Not only does He make peace in a strange way, it is also a strange peace. It is not just peace but "*My* peace I give to you." He gives it "not as the world gives" because that is a different sort of peace. It is not the peace we expect, not a sort of comfortable niceness. Jesus was not nice. Jesus was not an uncle. Jesus was a fire. "I come not to bring peace but a sword" (this refers to the world's peace). Yet "peace I leave with you" (this refers to His peace). The explanation of the paradox is that the sword He brings is not the world's sword (most of us understand that) and the peace He brings is not the world's peace (many of us do *not* understand that).

What sword did He bring and how did this make peace?

The sword was not a physical one. Peter's sword was ordered back into its sheath and should have stayed there for the next two thousand years. The *jihad,* "holy war," is not a Christian idea but a heretical one. It is taught by one of the great Christian heresies,

Islam. How ironic it is that the religion with the name that means "peace" and "surrender" (*Islam* is cognate to *shalom*) should justify the holy war! And how ironic it is that so many wars have been fought in the name of the Prince of Peace, many of them wars of Christians against Christians. Saint Paul was scandalized even by lawsuits of Christian against Christian (see 1 Corinthians 6). How much more would he feel a holy horror at our war-stained history! Those who sing "Onward, Christian soldiers" have often forgotten that "we do not wrestle against flesh and blood, but against principalities, against powers" (Eph. 6:12).

Yet Christ brought a kind of sword and said so: "I have come to set a man against his father, a daughter against her mother" (Matt. 10:35). No one in history ever generated more passion and controversy, more opposition and more enemies. No one was ever more loved, and no one was ever more hated. And if we do not understand both halves of that paradox, we do not understand Christ.

His whole life on earth was associated with violence, from Bethlehem's slaughtered innocents to Calvary's crucified thieves. His own experience was full of spiritual warfare, from the temptation in the wilderness to the agony in the garden. The traditional metaphor of the Christian life as a warfare is not optional, not dispensable, but necessary, for it comes not from the social customs of a militaristic mentality but from the will of God, from the life of Christ, and from His own words.

It was in and through this spiritual warfare that He made spiritual peace, peace between man and God. From that ultimate peace comes the other peace, peace between man and man. In our history it has been so. Not politics but sanctity abolished barbarism and slavery and snobbery. It is the long way round, but it is the surgeon's only way, to deal with the root cause of the disease, not just the symptoms.

This is why Saint Paul did not tell slaves to rebel against their masters, and why the early church did not fight a civil war to emancipate slaves, and why we should not bomb abortion clinics. It simply wouldn't work. A merely political abolition of slavery, desirable as it obviously is, would destroy only slavery's flower, not its root in the human heart, the desire to enslave; and that root would grow new flowers of evil.

There is no shorter, better way than Christ's to make peace. The temptation is to be content with short-range peace, immediate peace, peace in the symptoms, and even to sacrifice truth and justice and honesty and religious integrity for "peace at any price." This is, of course, a false peace, and the prophet exposed it when he cried woe to those who cry "'Peace, peace!' When there is no peace" (Jer. 6:14). The truth will inevitably sound utterly unacceptable and scandalous to the world and provoke not peace but opposition; but the only way to true peace is to become a child of God in Christ. For peace is "rest in our end," and our end is God, and "no one comes to the Father except by Me" (John 14:6).

Narrow is the way to peace, and to life. Perhaps when the world is weary of alternatives it will turn to the narrow way, if it's still there after trying the alternatives. Meanwhile, you can do more to save the world from nuclear war than any politician or weapons system can. For peacemaking Christ's way is soul-winning. Spread the good infection of Christ, by word and deed of love, and if enough of us cast enough votes for peace every day, we will be blessed with it.

CHAPTER ELEVEN

Hungering for Righteousness vs. Satisfied with Sloth

SLOTH

Of all the Seven Deadly Sins, sloth is the most distinctively modern. Nothing so clearly distinguishes modern Western society from all previous societies as its sloth.

That claim sounds absurd in view of the fact that we are a busy, fussing, fidgety, anxious, fast-moving, success-worshiping, performance-oriented, Martha-type society, replete with ulcers, nervous breakdowns, and suicides. But at least we are hard-working. We have the grossest national product. How can anyone say we are lazy?

I did not say we are lazy. I said we are slothful.

Saint Thomas defines sloth as "sorrow about spiritual good," or joylessness when faced with God as our supreme joy. He explains that this is matter for mortal sin because it is a sin against charity. To understand this, we must remember that charity is one of the three theological virtues, or dispositions of the soul in regard to God, which attaches us to God. Faith, hope, and charity are our spiritual glue. Whatever dissolves this glue is mortally sinful; whatever can remove faith, hope, or charity can kill God's life in our soul. And sloth does just that.

How? By robbing us of our appetite for God, our zest for God,

149

our interest and enjoyment in God. Sloth stops us from seeking God, and that means we do not find Him. When Jesus said that all who seek, find, He implied that those who do not seek, do not find. Pascal put it this way: "There are three kinds of people in the world: those who have sought God and have found Him and now serve Him, those who are seeking Him but have not yet found Him, and those who neither seek Him nor find Him. The first are reasonable and happy, the second reasonable and unhappy, the third unreasonable and unhappy."

The big distinction, the eternal divide, is not between those who have found God and those who have not, but between those who seek Him and those who do not. For all seekers find; everyone in the second class eventually gets into the first, according to our Lord's own promise. Sloth is a mortal sin because it puts us into the third class.

Sloth is the most depressing thing in the world. It is Hell on earth. It finds our very highest joy, God Himself, joyless. If Joy Himself is joyless, where can we find joy? If the salt has lost its saltiness, how can it be restored? If the very light in us is darkness, how great is that darkness!

It may seem strange to define a mortal sin as a kind of sorrow, for sorrow is in itself only a feeling, and feelings are neither good nor evil. But sloth is our applying this feeling to something, to our highest end. Feelings come *to* me, and I am not directly responsible for their coming; but I am responsible for their going, for what I do with them, inwardly as well as outwardly. When I am sorrowful about my divine good, when my soul says no to God's offer of supreme joy, when I return His invitation ticket to His banquet, I am spiritually dead.

Sloth is a cold sin, not a hot one; but that makes it even deadlier. Rebellion against God is closer to Him than indifference is, just as hatred is closer to love than indifference is. God can more easily cool our wrath than fire our frozenness, though He can do both.

Sloth is a sin of omission, not commission. That too makes it deadlier, for a similar reason. To commit evil is at least to be playing the game, the only game in town, the game God is playing, though it is to play for the wrong side. But you can switch sides more easily than you can switch games. As Kierkegaard pointed out, the great enemy of morality today is not immorality but amorality (what he called the "aesthetic" attitude). Sloth simply does not play God's game, either with Him or against Him. It sits on the sidelines bored while life and death are at stake. Out with it! Better be God's enemy than a clod. Better either hot or cold than lukewarm. If that seems harsh, it is God's word, not mine, and He used an even more unflattering expression than "clod" in Revelation 3:16: "vomit."

Sloth is not just laziness. There are two kinds of laziness, the first of which is only mildly, or venially sinful, the second not a sin at all. Not working, or not working hard, at good and necessary earthly tasks is a minor sin. Preferring the pleasures of resting to the sweat of needed labor is irresponsible and self-indulgent; but it is not the mortal sin of sloth. Sloth refuses to work at our *heavenly* task.

The second kind of laziness belongs to a phlegmatic or slow temperament, such as is associated with the lifestyle of hot climates. "It's a lazy afternoon in summer" is a kind of delight, and sloth has no delight. Relaxing is not sloth. The person who never relaxes is not a saint but a fidget.

Ironically, it is often just such a fidget who is guilty of sloth. And here at last we are ready to clear up the paradoxical claim made at the beginning, that activistic modernity is slothful, by asking the obvious but seldom-asked question: *Why* are we so busy? Why, in this great age of time-saving devices, does no one have any free time? Why, now that we have technology to do our labor, is life emptier of leisure than it ever was in pretechnological societies? What are we hiding from ourselves with all this pointless and un-happifying activism?

We are hiding ourselves; we are hiding the God-sized hole in our hearts, the hole in the foundation of our existence. We try to paper the hole over with a thousand things, but they are all thin, and we know we will fall through the hole if we get too close. So we don't. We avoid God's absence as much as God's presence. We are slothful.

There is a deep spiritual sorrow at the heart of modern civiliza-tion because it is the first civilization in all of history that does not know who it is or why it is, that cannot answer the three great questions: Where did I come from? Why am I here? and Where am I going?

This is the most terrifying thing of all to us, because our pri-mary need is denied, our need for meaning. This terror is so great that it must be pushed down far into the unconscious by sloth, or we would go insane. So we cover it up with a thousand busynesses. Thus, paradoxically, it is our very sloth that produces our frantic activism.

Our lust is also a cover-up for sloth. Saint Thomas explains in the *Summa* how "something arises from sorrow in two ways: first, that man shuns whatever causes sorrow, secondly, that he turns to other things that give him pleasure: thus those who find no joy in spiritual pleasures [that is sloth] turn to pleasures of the body [lust]." As Walker Percy puts its, since modern man fears he is a ghost, he has to assure himself of his reality by lust. Ghosts don't get erections.

The familiar face of sloth in our world can be identified from Saint Thomas's further description of it as "an oppressive sorrow

which so weighs upon a man's mind that he wants to do nothing."
Sound familiar? It's a pretty exact, clinical description of what we
call depression. It is a symptom or effect of boredom.

Now why are we bored? Why this distinctively modern phenomenon? The very *word* for it did not exist in premodern lan-
guages! Above all, how do we explain the irony that the very
society which for the first time in history has conquered nature by
technology and turned the world into a giant fun-and-games fac-
tory, a rich kid's playroom, the very society which has the least
reason to be bored, is the most bored? Why is an American child
playing with ten thousand dollars worth of video equipment more
bored than an Indian child playing with two sticks and a stone?

The answer is inescapable. There is only one thing that never
gets boring: God. The God-shaped vacuum in us is infinite and
cannot be filled with any finite objects or actions. Therefore if we
are bored with God, we will be bored with everything. For as Saint
Augustine says, he who has God has everything; he who has
everything but God has nothing; and he who has God plus everything else does not have any more than he who has God alone.

Modern man has sloth, that is, sorrow about God, because
God is dead to him. He is the cosmic orphan. Nothing can take
the place of his dead Father; all idols fail, and bore. When God is
dead, it is the time of the twilight of the gods as well.

Pascal describes modernity's slothful attitude toward the great
spiritual questions in his *Pensées:*

> How can such an argument as this occur to a reasonable man?
> 'I do not know who put me into the world . . . nor what I am
> myself. . . . All I know is that I must soon die, but what I know
> least about is this very death which I cannot evade.
>
> Just as I do not know whence I come, so I do not know whither I
> am going. . . . And my conclusion from all this is that I must pass

my days without a thought of seeking what is to happen to me. Perhaps I might find some enlightenment in my doubts, but I do not want to take the trouble, nor take a step to look for it; and afterwards, as I sneer at those who are striving to this end . . . I will go without fear or foresight to face so momentous an event, and allow myself to be carried off limply to my death, uncertain of my future state for all eternity.'

Who would wish to have as his friend a man who argued like that? Who would choose him from among others as a confidant in his affairs? Who would resort to him in adversity? To what use in life could he possibly be turned?

It is truly glorious for religion to have such unreasonable men as enemies. . . . the same man who spends so many days and nights in fury and despair at losing some office or at some imaginary affront to his honor is the very one who knows that he is going to lose everything through death but feels neither anxiety nor emotion. It is a monstrous thing to see one and the same heart at once so sensitive to minor things and so strangely insensitive to the greatest. It is an incomprehensible spell, a supernatural torpor. . . .[1]

It is sloth. A second great observer of it is Kierkegaard:

Let others complain that the age is wicked; my complaint is that it is wretched, for it lacks passion. Men's thoughts are thin and flimsy like lace, they are themselves pitiable like the lacemakers. The thoughts of their hearts are too paltry to be sinful. For a worm it might be regarded as a sin to harbor such thoughts, but not for a being made in the image of God. Their lusts are dull and sluggish, their passions sleepy. They do their duty, these shopkeeping souls, but they clip the coin a trifle . . . they think that even if the Lord keeps ever so careful a set of books, they may still cheat Him a little. Out upon them! This is the reason my soul always turns back to the Old Testament and to Shakespeare. I feel that those who speak there are at least human beings; they hate, they love, they murder their enemies and curse their descendants throughout all generations, they sin.[2]

Sloth is the sin that is so dead that it doesn't even seem to rise to the level of sin, the sin so sinful that it isn't even sin.

One reason modernity is so victimized by sloth is its preference for toleration over truth, its fear of religious passions and the religious wars that it (wrongly) traces to them. But the Western world is under absolutely no danger of religious war, despite hysterical cries from secularists and ACLU types. We simply lack the passion, especially the passion for truth. The danger in earlier ages was anger; ours is sloth, indifference, and depression.

But don't we have a right to be depressed in the modern world? It's a depressing world! Only a fool gets passionate about drains or cosmetics or mufflers. Only an idiot never gets bored with economics and politics. Better bored in such a world than fascinated. At least rise above the inanities of pop psychology to the dignity of despair.

Yes, surely. But the most crucial fact of all is forgotten: God is still here. The world God created *cannot* be secularized, only man's consciousness can. God does not die, He is only eclipsed. As Saint Thomas More said, "The times are never so bad but that a good man can live in them." No, we do *not* have a right to our depression, because God is here, the God who spoke in the Big Bang and the burning bush and the Resurrection: "Lo, I am with you always, even to the end of the age" (Matt. 28:20).

The cure for depression and sloth is simply faith, affirmation of the God who is here, acceptance of God's offer of Himself. No, something even less than faith will do. Faith is finding, but mere seeking overcomes sloth. For seeking becomes finding, and finding becomes joy, and joy overcomes sloth.

Seeking means hungering. Thus the beatitude that confronts sloth is the one about hungering.

"Blessed are those who hunger and thirst for righteousness, for they shall be filled."

Not everyone hungers for righteousness, but everyone hungers. Everybody's looking for something. Hunger is our very nature. Our souls, like our bodies, need food. No one but God is self-sufficient.

Not only humanity but everything in creation has a hunger, for nothing but God is self-sufficient. That is another way of saying that only God is eternal, and all of creation moves through time because it is hungering for something it has not yet, or is not yet.

On the physical level, this hunger is gravity. Science has not explained *why* matter moves, why matter attracts matter, only *how*. The answer to *why* is love, "the love that moves the sun and all the stars" (Dante). Love is the secret of gravity. Even matter hungers. But the motion here is wholly external. Each bit of matter is moved not by itself but by another bit of matter.

When we cross the line dividing the inorganic from the organic, we find a different kind of hunger. Plants grow from within. They hunger not just to move in space but to move toward their own perfection, growth, and maturity.

When we climb the chain of being to the animal world, we find another kind of hunger—consciousness—in the form of instincts and feelings about other animals and things.

Finally, man is self-moved in that he has free choice and free will, as well as gravity, growth, and instincts. His mind hungers for truth, his will for goodness (righteousness), and his imagination and emotions for beauty.

What about God? Does he hunger? Yes and no. God has no needs, and therefore no need-loves. The reason is not that God lacks love but that God *is* love. Water can't get wet because it *is* wet. God can't "fall" in love because he *is* love. This love is *agapē*, gift-love, love based on excess, not defect. God is like an overflowing fountain, not like a receiving bucket. But this fountain is no less dynamic, demanding, active, and alarming than our most passionate need-loves. The Hound of Heaven hunts for us more assiduously than a starving dog hunts for a steak.

God too hungers and thirsts. He told us so, from the cross. It was not vinegar He thirsted for, but for people to enter His Kingdom. Lovers thirst for other selves, not to consume but to give themselves to.

We have four hungers: The first we share with the lower creation for it pertains to the physical. Second, our human spirit has a natural hunger for its kind of food, truth, goodness, and beauty. Third, our spirit's center, that spiritual organ Scripture calls the "heart," hungers for God, knowingly or unknowingly. That's why no one is ever completely happy here, why even after Bach, even after Plato, even after Shakespeare, we say: "Is that all there is?" Fourth, we can also share *God's* hunger, *agapē*'s hunger to spend itself, give itself. This *(agapē) is* righteousness, the very nature of God's goodness itself. Our third hunger is the hunger for the source of this righteousness, God, explicitly or implicitly known. And our second hunger is the hunger for the effect, or gift, given by God, goodness again, known or unknown, explicit or implicit.

Even when fools mistake something else for this true good, the homing pigeon in the soul drives them away from the false goods by souring their joy and stirring up their "divine discontent." God has left the great grace of unhappiness even to the most foolish and lost souls as a warning signal to turn them toward home. Like

E.T., they can't find their way home, and they are lonely. We must help them home.

The "righteousness" Jesus speaks of in this beatitude, then, is that which comes from the very nature of God. It is not merely legal justice but holiness, goodness, God-ness, likeness to God. And that means *agapē,* for "God is *agapē.*"

Now comes the wonderful news: all seekers find. If righteousness is what you really want, you will infallibly find it, sooner or later, in God's time and in God's way. It's guaranteed. Only the best things in life are free. Only the best thing of all is absolutely guaranteed: God himself. The reason for this is simple: God is love, and love is generous, wanting to give, needing only cooperation on the part of the recipient in the form of willing, wanting, hungering. Thus all who hunger for God's righteousness will be filled with it.

Saint Alphonsus Liguori says we can look forward to death if we hunger and thirst for righteousness, because after death we cannot sin any more, and sin is the only obstacle to the righteousness we long for. Just imagine, no more selfishness, no more cowardice, no more lust, no more dishonesty, no more foolishness, no more hardness of heart, no more weakness of will. If we hunger for goodness, we can look forward to the golden door of death.

But *do* we hunger for goodness? Everyone hungers to receive good, but not everyone hungers to give good, for not everyone knows that "it is more blessed to give than to receive." Not everyone prays Saint Francis's wise prayer, knowing that "it is in giving that we receive." Why is it that not everyone knows this? Because we know this only by faith. Thus faith is the root of the hunger for righteousness.

How can we test whether or not we hunger and thirst for righteousness and thus know whether or not we are guaranteed to be filled? How can we find out if we want most to love or only to be loved, to give or only to receive, whether our fundamental option is obedience to the first and greatest commandment, to love the Lord our God with our whole heart and mind and soul? Although none of us keeps that high and holy commandment, how can we know that we *want* to keep it more than we want anything else, that we want most of all to give God our heart, that we hunger and thirst for righteousness most of all?

Saint Augustine, in one of his sermons, invents a wonderful device, a kind of psychodrama, to test ourselves. Imagine God coming to you and offering you the following bargain: God offers to give you everything you can imagine in this world and the next as well. Nothing shall be impossible to you and nothing shall be forbidden. There will be no sin, no guilt. Anything you imagine can be yours. There is only one thing you will have to give up: You shall never see My face, says God.

Now if you do not love God above all things, why was there that terrible chill in your heart when you heard those last words? If you would not accept this bargain, look what you just did: You gave up the whole world for God.

But, you may object, this does not test whether my basic desire is to give or to get, just whether I want to get the world or to get God. Not so, for no one can *get* God. Union with the world can be by getting, by having, by possession. But union with God can be only by giving yourself to God, by God's getting you. So if you want God, you want to give yourself to God. God has already given Himself to you, by the unthinkable generosity of creation, incarnation, and redemption. The only open question is whether you give yourself in return, whether you hunger to be possessed.

Those of us who do not, who are satisfied with ninety years of riches and comfort, are doomed, like Dives. How blessed is Lazarus by contrast! How blessed is poverty, suffering, and anything that destroys the most deadly thing in the world, the quiet drift to

Hell! Dissatisfaction is the second best thing there is, because it dissolves the glue that entraps us to false satisfactions, and drives us to God, the only true satisfaction. The road home is the next best thing to home. God is home and dissatisfaction is the road, hunger and thirst for God is the road. Blessed are those who hunger and thirst for God's righteousness, for they shall be filled.

CHAPTER TWELVE

Pure of Heart vs.
Lustful of Heart

LUST

O.K., gang, here's the one you've all been waiting for, the one really *interesting* sin!

Everyone knows our society is sex-obsessed, sex-saturated. If lust ceased tomorrow, we would be plunged into the greatest economic depression in history. Remove sex appeal from advertising, advertising from the economy, and the economy from our civilization, and what would be left?

But ours is only an extreme form today of a perennial phenomenon. It did not take Freud or Hugh Hefner to discover that lust is fun. Even Saint Thomas Aquinas noted that "lust . . . is about the greatest of pleasures, and these absorb the mind more than any others."

But when we turn to the great spiritual masters, we find a surprising soberness about lust. With some exceptions (like Saint Jerome), they do not share our obsession ("You mean there are six other deadly sins too?"). They neither fixate on it nor excuse it. They neither call it the greatest sin nor the least.

It is not the most serious sin—pride is that—because it is usually a sin of weakness, of the flesh, not of the Devil or even the world, at least not immediately. Jesus spent much more time warning us against temptations from the world (avarice, human respect) and from the Devil (pride, hypocrisy) than from the flesh.

We often think sexual sins must be the greatest ones because they promise the greatest pleasures. But this is a Stoic or Kantian viewpoint, not a Christian one. For God, not the Devil, invented sex, and pleasure, and the connection between the two. In fact, Saint Thomas says that sexual pleasure was even greater before the Fall, because the fallen and unnatural can never give as much pleasure as the unfallen and natural.

But lust *is* a sin. More exactly, it is the desire for the sins of fornication or adultery (a desire in the will, not just the feelings, something actively consented to, not just passively experienced). Jesus clearly said that the desire for adultery *is* adultery: "Whoever looks at a woman to lust for her has already committed adultery with her in his heart" (Matt. 5:28).

Yet many people today believe that even the act of fornication, much less the desire, couldn't be sinful, and therefore neither could lust, "because it doesn't hurt anybody." Saint Thomas long ago refuted that argument, that "simple fornication is not contrary to charity because no one is injured by it," by pointing out that fornication "is contrary to the love of our neighbor because it is opposed to the good of the child to be born," and that it is a sufficiently weighty matter for mortal sin because "every sin committed directly against human life is a mortal sin." Nevertheless full consent of the will is usually suppressed by the overriding passion of the moment in Christians, who know God's law, and by ignorance in non-Christians. Saint Thomas says, "The sinner is freed from eternal loss when it is done out of weakness rather than impenitence."

It may be that, as the famous Fatima message says, more souls go to Hell because of this sin than any other. But that does not mean this is the worst sin, only the most popular. Do not confuse quantity with quality. It may be the widest road but it is not the deepest pit.

We often define lust either too narrowly or too broadly, and both can be convenient ways of denying our guilt. We can define it so narrowly that we are seldom guilty of it by suggesting that lust means only treating a person of the opposite sex (let me say woman, since I am a man; women can reverse the polarity) as an object or thing rather than as a subject or person. Lust then becomes the attitude a married man might have toward a prostitute but not toward a mistress. By this definition infidelity is not lust as long as the adulterer felt "love" for his mistress. Such a definition conveniently forgets the wife, just as the concept of abortion as "a matter between a woman and her doctor" conveniently forgets the father—and the baby.

Alternatively, we could define lust so broadly that it is no sin at all, for example, the notion that lust means any great passion, like a "lust for life" or a "lust for learning." By this definition, all the saints lusted for God!

Another overextension of the term is one that calls any sexual desire "lust." But lust is a sin and sexual desire as such is not. It is God's invention and implied in His very first command to our race, "Be fruitful and multiply." God did not mean: Learn the multiplication tables! Nor did Adam and Eve grow children like plants until the Fall. Their desire for each other was subject to reason; but contrary to modern prejudice, this does not mean that reason annihilated it or took the fun out of it.

Not only is sexual desire not sinful, it is sometimes a moral obligation. A husband and wife *should* have it for each other, and consciously cultivate it, by licit means and in the context of personal love and respect. Saint Thomas even notes that there is a contrary vice to lust, though it is rare: insensibility or aversion to sex.

Another too-broad conception of lust is the spontaneous appreciation of the sexual beauty of another woman. The involuntary turn of the head to notice and be pleased with her beauty is not lust. Desiring and planning adultery with her is. So is deliberately fantasizing about it. So, even, is deliberately conjuring up the pleasure of the first look once again just for the sake of getting the pleasure, though this is a very mild fault compared with the other two. All three are forms of adultery in the heart. But not noticing is a form of insensibility. Unfortunately, the leap between noticing and lusting, between the first and the second look, is often small and easily made.

The ancient Greek philosophers often saw the harm in lust in rationalistic terms, in the harm done to the mind and judgment by the beclouding effect of lust. This is not Scripture's approach. What matters, according to the bare bones of the sixth commandment, is simply *whom* you have intercourse with, or desire to have it with. The Greek idea is too individualistic, even selfish. The luster harms his own rational perfection, but what about his neighbor? What about his wife? What about his children? It is an idea only philosophers ever bought.

Yet there is a truth in it. Lust *does* addict and blind the mind. That "Love is blind" *is* true of lust, but it is not true of *agapē*, unless God is blind! One of the following three statements *must* be false: (1) God is not blind, (2) God is love, (3) Love is blind.

The most important thing to know about lust is how to avoid it. Since it is the most popular sin, both the most attractive and the most widespread, any workable advice on overcoming it would seem pretty rare and valuable. "Try a little harder" is about as effective as an ice cube in a furnace. What else is there?

First, remember a principle of God's grace which we saw in exploring pride: God often withholds from us the grace to avoid a lesser sin because we are in danger of a greater sin. To avoid pride, He sometimes lets us fall into lust, since lust is usually obvious, undisguised, and temporary, while pride is not. So to conquer lust, we should focus less on lust and more on pride. Only when we are truly humble does God give us the grace to conquer lust.

Second, remember Saint Thomas's diagnosis of lust, which I think he must have learned from Saint Augustine: "Man cannot live without joy; therefore when he is deprived of true spiritual joys it is necessary that he become addicted to carnal pleasures." God is not a substitute for sex, as Freud thought; sex is often a substitute for God. The passionate gravity of the soul is meant for God. When the true God comes, the false gods go. To conquer lust, forget about lust and love God.

Third, we must lay the axe to the root by operating on our very thoughts, as Saint Paul advises, "bringing every thought into captivity to Christ." We need a good brainwashing. Brainwashing is not propaganda; brain-dirtying is propaganda. Our thoughts are wild animals; only Christ can tame them. All we can do, all we need to do, is bring them to Him—immediately.

Thought is the rudder of life. As the poet Samuel Smiles says:

> Sow a thought, reap an act.
> Sow an act, reap a habit.
> Sow a habit, reap a character.
> Sow a character, reap a destiny.

Buddha begins his most famous work, the *Dhammapada,* with the line: "All that we are is dependent on our thoughts. It begins with our thoughts, it continues with our thoughts, it ends with our thoughts." The body is a dumb and innocent little donkey. The worst that can be said of it is that it is lazy and stubborn at times. It is his rider, Thought, who keeps turning him wrong.

Fourth, we must realize that lust is an addiction and treat it as such. As Terence said, "You cannot control it by counseling."

Plato was wrong; evil is not only ignorance and curable by reason, education, or good advice. Saint Paul discovered the mysterious gap between knowing the good and doing it when he wrote: "What I am doing, I do not understand. . . . The good that I will to do, I do not do; but the evil I will not to do, that I practice" (Rom. 7:15, 19).

So what is the practical solution to this addiction? Saint Paul tells us immediately: "Who will deliver me from this body of death? I thank God—through Jesus Christ our Lord!" (7:24–25) The only solution is supernatural. Not knowing this leads to either presumption (if we think we can do it alone) or despair (if we know we can't), or both. Saint Augustine recounts in his *Confessions* how he "hesitated to enroll in Your army" because he knew himself too well to think he could fulfill God's law of chastity: "I could not live without the embraces of a woman." He did not know the remedy God provided: grace. When he came to know that, he prayed, "Give what Thou commandest, and then command what Thou wilt."

"It's *all* grace," said Saint Theresa. Saint Philip Neri's remark about the beggar is literally true for all of us: "There but for the grace of God go I." And that is why Brother Lawrence says, in *The Practice of the Presence of God,* that after he falls into any sin he simply repents, says to God, "See? That's what I shall always do when You do not give me the grace!" and then goes on, not fixated on the past. It sounds cavalier, but sometimes God's solutions are tenderer than ours. Perhaps always.

This brings me to my fifth and last piece of practical advice. It is culled from the Akathist Hymn used by Eastern rite churches. The Virgin Mary is hailed in a hundred beautiful ways in this hymn, including this one: "Hail, tenderness vanquishing all desire."

Not insensitivity, not impersonal rationality, not brute will power, but loving tenderness, sister-love, mother-love, something close to the heart of Love itself, is stronger than the whirling circles of love's outer perversions. The Lamb of tenderness vanquishes the Beast of desire in us just as He does in Revelation. And from the cross He gave to His beloved disciple, John, and through him to the Church and ourselves, His mother, the mother of tenderness, a "tenderness vanquishing all desire." The example of Mary is supremely relevant to our lust-laden century.

**"Blessed are the pure in heart,
for they shall see God."**

Lust is like mud. Its opposite is like clear water, or clean air. It is called purity of heart. Purity's most obvious aspect is sexual, as confronting sexual lust. But it is much more than that. It must be, for its reward is much more than the reward of only sexual purity. A tyrant or a devil-inspired fanatic can have sexual purity, but can not have Jesus' purity of heart.

Let us explore what purity of heart is by looking first at its reward.

It is the greatest reward of all. "To see God," that is joy, the fulfillment of everyone's deepest desire, whether they know it or not. "This is eternal life, to know Thee." Just to know. For this "knowing" is not just abstract doctrine but concrete experience. It satisfies not curiosity but love. It is the kind of knowledge husband and wife have of each other: "And Adam knew his wife Eve"— and the product was not a book but a baby. When they had "known" good and evil, the product was not a sermon on ethics, but spiritual divorce from God, death. This knowing is literally a matter of life or death.

We are promised the great and inconceivable gift to see God face to face, as He is, just as Enoch, Moses, and Job did. It is "the

Beatific Vision," "the spiritual marriage," something "Eye has not seen, nor ear heard,/Nor have entered into the heart of man,/ The things which God has prepared for those who love Him (1 Cor. 2:9). This is Home. It is what we were made for, our "pearl of great price," our "one thing necessary." If we only knew, we would eagerly sacrifice anything and everything in the world for this.

This beatitude answers two questions: What is our ultimate end? and What is our means to that end? We must explain the connection between the means and the end. Seeing God is our end, our home; what is the way?

"I am the way," says Jesus. But in the beatitude, purity of heart is the way. Is there a contradiction here? No, for Jesus *is* our purity of heart.

First, Jesus alone gives purity of heart, for purity of heart simply cannot be attained by fallen human nature. The physician cannot heal himself, the leopard cannot change its spots. Purity of heart is a divine attribute and can be attained only by divine power, divine grace: Christ.

Second, Jesus not only *gives* purity of heart, but Jesus *is* our purity of heart. "God has made Him to *be* our righteousness." He does not dispense grace like pills; He *is* grace. God's solution to our problems is not to send down a spiritual jack-of-all-trades, a fixit man to patch our leaks and put little gifts under our tree. Grace is not like little sparks of electricity spun off from the divine dynamo into millions of receiving sets. Rather, God puts us into Christ, incorporates us into the new race, the Mystical Body of Christ. There, grace comes not from without but from within; there, grace is nature.

God's single solution to all our problems is Jesus Christ. We attain purity of heart not merely by the imitation *of* Christ but by the incorporation *into* Christ, the Christ who has perfect purity of heart, the Christ whose only will is to do the will of the Father.

For that is what purity of heart is. In the words of Kierkegaard's simple and memorable title, "Purity Of Heart Is to Will One Thing." *Pure* means "authentic, simple, wholly itself, true." The Hebrew word for it is *emeth*, "truth." Pure, true water is all H_2O, not part chlorine. Pure gold is unalloyed. A pure will loves God with the whole heart and soul and mind. It is "fanatical," the greatest insult the modern mind can conceive, and the greatest compliment God can give.

It is also the greatest compliment a lover can give: "I love you with my whole heart and soul. My love is not divided. You have no rival." Only love understands the rightness of this fanaticism, and through it the wrongness of all other, lesser fanaticisms. The loveless or paltry lover cannot understand *why* lesser fanaticisms are wrong because he does not understand why the great fanaticism is right. Counterfeits are comprehensible only in the light of the authentic article; only the worshiper of the true God knows why idols are idols.

If God were to appear to me this minute and offer me any one of His graces, this is the one I would ask for: purity of heart, to will one thing, to obey the first and greatest commandment. First things first. Purity of heart means total love, being like God, Who *is* total love.

All our evils, spiritual and physical, sins and consequent sufferings, are due to our lack of purity of heart. If we did not have divided and impure hearts, we would love God wholly, and nothing bad can come from that. "Love and do what you will," Augustine said.

The immediate result of the Fall was that we no longer loved God wholeheartedly. Sin's first effect is here, in the organ in which it originated, in the heart: separation from God and God's will, which is the root and essence of sin. The immediate result is separation from self, a tear in our heart, a divided heart. Saints experience it as much as sinners. Indeed, though they have it less, they feel it more. They cry in agony, "I do not understand my own actions. For I do not do what I want, but I do the very thing I hate" (Rom. 7:15 RSV). What a mystery the mystery of iniquity is! How dark to the reason as well as to the will! How precious the alternative, purity of heart!

The most important question about purity of heart is the practical question, how we get this priceless pearl. The answer, of course, is by God's grace, that is, by Christ. Our need for purity of heart prods us toward Christ, as does everything else, if we listen. Christ is the point, the end, to which all our experience leads. Christ must be all in all.

What is the connection between this virtue and its reward, between purity of heart and seeing God? Why is purity of heart the only way to see God?

It is not that God has decided to arrange it that way as a reward system, but of an intrinsic necessity. In no possible way, in no possible world, could we see God without purity of heart, any more than two plus two could equal three, or injustice could be better than justice. It's not that God makes a little deal with us and says, "Unless you come up to the standards I've set, unless you follow My rules, I won't let you see Me." Rather, in the very nature of things we cannot see God without purity of heart, just as we cannot see colors without eyes.

We cannot see God until our heart is like an eagle instead of an owl, able to see the sun. Here is the point of life and of morality: to grow eagles' eyes. Our lives are a process of growing the necessary organs for our destiny. That is the reason why God is such a stickler about morality, not because He wants to control our behavior, but because He wants us to become the kind of people who can see Him and thus experience infinite joy. Morality knows how to love and how to become lovable. Love longs to spend itself, longs to give itself to a perfected beloved. We must learn to be holy to satisfy God's desire, Love's desire, to spend itself on us.

Paradoxically, this growing process is a shrinking process. Growing into spiritual maturity, into the kind of creatures God can love more and more, means shrinking our idolatries, purifying our love. Thus this beatitude is intimately connected with the first, poverty of spirit or detachment. Both are like radiation therapy to shrink cancerous tissue.

The psychology implied in the sixth beatitude is Hebrew rather than Greek. In classical Greek philosophy, head rules heart, reason rules will. In Scripture, it is reversed. The heart of man is not the head but the heart, the prefunctional root of all psychic functions, including reason, understanding, wisdom. "Keep your heart with all diligence, for out of it spring the issues of life," says Solomon (Prov. 4:23).

The Greek psychology is the correct one for science, for knowing the world, for the I-It relationship, since the scientist cannot let his heart get in the way of his head, and you do not know a rock by loving it. But the biblical psychology is the correct one for the I-Thou relationship. The only way really to know a person, human or divine, is by the heart, by love. Who knows you best, the detached but brilliant psychologist for whom you are a three-volume case study, or your not-too-bright friend who loves you truly and deeply?

Thus when His critics demand of Jesus how they can know where He gets His wisdom and authority, from God or from man, Jesus answers: "My doctrine is not Mine, but His who sent Me.

If anyone wants to do His will, he shall know concerning the doctrine, whether it is from God or whether I speak on My own authority" (John 7:16–17).

First love the Father, then you will understand the teaching of the Son. First get your heart in line with God's heart, then your mind will line up with God's mind. First love and then you will understand. First be pure of heart and then you will see God.

This is the reason why it is saints, not scholars, who understand the Bible. It is God's word, and God is not an It but a Thou, or rather an I (*the* I). Scripture is a love letter, not a manual of scholastic theology. And only a lover understands a love letter. In fact, the Word of God is not first of all a book, but first of all a Person: an Author, not a publication. In the Holy Scriptures we are led once again to Christ the center. To the Pharisees, who stopped at the book, Jesus says: "You search the Scriptures, for in them you think you have eternal life; and these are they which testify of Me" (John 5:39). What an irony to prefer the letter to the lover, the picture to the person. It comes from preferring the head to the heart. But the head never brings purity of heart, while the heart brings purity of head. Jesus is single-minded because He is single-hearted. The lover sees the single-pointed, perfectly simple God Who is simply and purely Love itself, only with eyes which are purified by the heart.

CHAPTER THIRTEEN

Courage under Persecution vs. Self-indulgence (Gluttony)

GLUTTONY

Everyone knows what gluttony is: eating or drinking inordinately, contrary to reason. Medieval moralists distinguished five ways this could be done: hastily (gulping), sumptuously (demanding rich foods), excessively (too much), greedily (I want what I want when I want it) or daintily (it must be perfectly prepared).

The last category makes the point that the "just so" epicure may be just as gluttonous as the human hog and cause just as much trouble to others. The little old lady can be a glutton just as the redneck good ole boy, and not know it, which makes it more dangerous.

The medievals also listed five "daughters of gluttony": unseemly joy ("as though reason were fast asleep at the helm"), scurrility (foolish talk and behavior), uncleanness (vomiting), loquaciousness (immoderate speech), and dullness of mind as regards the understanding "on account of the fumes of food disturbing the brain."

Before we laugh patronizingly and return these lists to the museum, perhaps we should recall that cookbooks outsell Bibles in this most Bible-reading of all countries of the world by something like ten to one.

But surely gluttony is the least serious of the Seven Deadly Sins? It seems even to be the one the clergy is most (happily) addicted to, as evidenced by the following Jewish joke. A Jewish couple wanted to know what their son would be when he grew up. So they asked their rabbi for advice. "Put him in a room," the rabbi said, "with nothing but one table. Put on the table a soufflé, a bottle of whiskey, a roll of money, and a Bible. If he picks up the soufflé, he'll be an epicure. If he picks up the whiskey, he'll be an alcoholic. If he picks up the money, he'll be a businessman. And if he picks up the Bible, he'll be a rabbi." The next day the parents returned to the rabbi. "What happened?" he asked. "We don't understand," the parents said. "He ate the soufflé, drank the whiskey, put the money in his pocket, picked up the Bible, and came out. What does that mean?" "Oy, do I have bad news for you!" said the rabbi. "Your son is going to be a Jesuit!"

Saint Thomas agrees that gluttony is not one of the worst sins, and gives two reasons for this. First, its matter is only bodily food, not spiritual things; and second, "on account of the difficulty of proper discretion and moderation in such matters." It is a sin of the flesh, and sins of the flesh are perhaps more popular than spiritual sins, but not as deadly.

Yet this is one of the seven deadlies. It can be deadly, a mortal sin "by turning a man away from his last end," that is, "when he adheres to the pleasure of gluttony as his end, for the sake of which he despises God."

But this state is rarely seen. When a person turns his back on God, it's usually for pride, avarice, or lust, not for gluttony. Milton's Satan said, "better to reign in Hell than serve in Heaven," not "the food is better in Hell." Scrooge stashed away gold, not turkeys. We do not have strip teases with steak or potato pornography.

Yet here are five considerations that make gluttony a more serious sin than it has so far seemed to be.

First, drunkenness is a subspecies of gluttony. And the havoc wrought by alcoholism in our time, as in the past, can be measured only by tons of human tears. Lives and souls have been ruined by the thing that Scripture says God made "to gladden the heart of man." *Abusus non tollit usus* ("the abuse does not take away the use"). But the abuse has been horrendous.

Second, gluttony, whether of food or drink, is an addiction, and this is an element in all sin. We are all addicts to something, stuck like flies to flypaper, in love with something other than God that we just have to have. *Detachment* and *unworldliness* are words of scorn or incomprehension today rather than words of wisdom.

Third, there is a deep unwisdom, deep folly involved in gluttony, something more serious than an overfull stomach. It is the illusion that we can be made happy by cramming our inner emptiness, of body as of soul, full of the things of this world. It is a recipe for disappointment.

Fourth, our society is guilty of collective gluttony in its program to conquer (or rape) nature. Like King Midas, we have become rich, but nature poor. All we touch turns to gold, that is, goes cold and dead. Like food, we destroy it by assimilating it. Every physical good follows that pattern; only spiritual goods are increased and fulfilled by our union with them. We can't have our cake and eat it too, but we can have our love and share it too.

One way our society shows its gluttony is by its unconcern for God's good earth. Orthodox Christians have been strangely slow to get in the vanguard of the ecology movement, which is essentially Christian stewardship extended planet-wide. We seem to want to eat our planet's resources up.

Finally, gluttony is closely connected with at least two other deadly sins, avarice and lust. A sure way of possessing is to assimilate, to eat. And pornography reduces a person to a piece of meat. It even uses the language of the epicure.

What is the cure for gluttony?

Scripture's cure is not dieting but fasting. This is not to criticize all dieting, responsible dieting; but surely there is something more joyous, robust, right, and royal in the traditional alternation of feasting and fasting than in the changeless greyness of daily cottage cheese. Fasting, in addition to reducing weight, reduces gluttony and, best of all, is a form of prayer. It is recommended to us on the very highest authority, that of our Lord Himself.

But we must do more, not less. We must go to the root of the matter. The motivation for gluttony is the unconscious self-image of emptiness. I must fill myself because I am empty, ghostlike, worthless. Only a knowledge of God's love for me can fill that emptiness, make me a solid self, give me ultimate worth. And that knowledge comes through Jesus Christ. Therefore Jesus is the ultimate answer to gluttony, as to every other one of our problems. "My God shall supply all your needs . . . by Christ Jesus," Saint Paul assures us (Phil. 4:19).

In this as with all sin, direct attack usually doesn't work well. Concentrating on gluttony does not usually cure gluttony, especially in its serious stages, for it focuses attention on the very addiction or obsession that we want to escape. The same principle is true for lust. Though it sounds irresponsible and simplistic, we must "turn our back on our problem" and look to God as our joy, our end, our fulfillment, our all, for the simple reason that he is. It is not a trick of thought control but a fact, the primary fact of our being. He is our life, and sin is our death. But the deadliest of deadly sins is never as strong as God's burning fountain of joy. "Where sin abounded, grace abounded much more" (Rom. 5:20).

"Blessed are those who are persecuted for righteousness' sake, for
theirs is the Kingdom of Heaven. Blessed are you when they
revile and persecute you, and say all kinds of evil against you
falsely for My sake. Rejoice and be exceedingly glad, for great is
your reward in heaven, for so they persecuted the prophets who
were before you."

There are really eight beatitudes, not nine, but these last two are
usually counted as one, the eighth being a restatement and exten-
sion of the seventh.

The specific sin of gluttony and the specific grace of blessedness
under persecution confront each other. Gluttony is self-indulgence, the demand to have the world's real food for the stomach
and the world's false food for the soul. The beatitude of standing
fast under persecution is the strength of self-sacrifice. The contrast
is between getting and giving, between a gluttonous finding that is
really a losing and a martyr's losing that is really a finding.

The beatitude is another outrageous paradox, especially to our
collectivistic, conformistic age, when nearly everyone is terribly
concerned to be accepted by society, and in which therefore the
odium of ostracism inherent in persecution is feared almost as
much as the physical threats. An independent-minded person can
only be *physically* threatened and persecuted; but a conformist, a
compulsive joiner, can also be psychologically persecuted by ostracism.

And there is one thing that will always bring ostracism by the
world: unworldliness. Jesus guarantees that: "Because you are not
of the world, but I chose you out of the world, therefore the world
hates you. Remember the word that I said to you, 'A servant is not
greater than his master.' If they persecuted Me, they will also persecute you" (John 15:19–20).

There are segments of the world where you can find acceptance even if you are a pervert, a punk, a sadist, or a snob. The world can digest any food made of its own substance, grown in its own garden. But it simply cannot digest heavenly food. It will always vomit up Christ and His church as alien and threatening, or else it will try to tame Christ, humanize Christ, reinterpret Christ in socially acceptable, currently fashionable ways—*its* ways—so that it can digest the new sugar-covered pill.

When the church, the body of Christ, is persecuted, Christ is persecuted: "Inasmuch as you did it to one of the least of these My brethren, you did it to Me." And Christ will continue to be persecuted in His Body until the end of time, for the world will never be able to digest Christ, since He is not an ingredient in the world or its recipe. An index of the church's fidelity to her Master is her indigestibility. When the world accepts the church, the church is no longer the church. "Woe to you when all men speak well of you, for so did their fathers to the false prophets," Christ warns us. "If they kept My word, they will keep yours also." The saying is ironic; the world heard Christ's word so well that it betrayed and crucified Him.

But the world cannot win. Light comprehends darkness, but darkness does not comprehend light, says John in his great prologue. (*Comprehend* here means both "encompass" and "understand.") The world—the fallen world, the old order more or less under the dominion of Satan—is darkness. Christ is light. The darkness cannot put out the light even by crucifixion. Christ rose, and so does the church. Persecutions only strengthen the church, not weaken it. Where is the church stronger today: East Germany or West? Poland or France? Russia or Sweden? "The blood of the martyrs is the seed of the Church."

In a cruel and simple society, persecution takes a cruel and simple form. Christians are thrown to the lions, or into the Gulag. In a comfortable and complex society like ours, persecution is more insidious because it is masked. It is an attack on the mind, not the body. It takes place in the media, not the coliseum. We have a war of words, not of gladiators.

We should not resent persecution because we should not be surprised by it. We should not be surprised by it because Christ has promised it to us. And we should not be afraid of it because Christ has pronounced it blessed. It is blessed because it unites us with Christ and His holy unacceptability.

Christ was "unacceptable" to the world. Have you noticed how modern people don't use the words *right* and *wrong, good* and *evil* any more, but *acceptable* and *unacceptable,* or *appropriate* and *inappropriate?* Little Lancelot has just bullied, kicked, and foul-mouthed his little sister, and his teacher or psychologist has "shared her feelings" about Lancelot's behavior. She finds it "inappropriate." I wonder what word she would have used for Hitler.

But let us not be bitter. Christ accepts the world even though the world does not accept Christ. The light embraces the darkness even though the darkness does not embrace the light. The doctor accepts the patient even though the patient does not accept the doctor.

Why doesn't the patient accept the doctor? For the same reason Israel did not accept the prophets. The prophets preached repentance before Jesus preached salvation. Before the good news comes the bad news. Before the prognosis comes the diagnosis. Before the healing comes the realization of the disease. The world does not want to hear the good news because that means hearing first the bad news.

Instead of berating the world here, let's try to understand it. Nobody likes to hear bad news, spiritual or physical. Imagine that you refused to believe you were ill, whether for good reasons or bad. And imagine that your friends kept telling you you were desperately ill and needed surgery. Wouldn't you feel persecuted by them? And when we feel persecuted, the natural reaction is to hit back with the same weapon, to bounce back the offensive thing to the offender, to persecute.

Of course the world persecutes its prophets. They're a dash of cold water in the face, a waking up from a comfortable dream. If you feel comfortable in sin, if you have a deep personal stake in sinful habits, then you're naturally going to hate the offer of salvation and will persecute anyone who seems to threaten your sins. You don't want to be deprived of your beloved addictions.

All Christians are persecuted, but some more than others for two reasons. Either they live in an unusually evil environment (even ordinary Christians are persecuted in the Soviet Union) or they are unusually good Christians. When Good meets Evil, the result is a Cross.

Most of us aren't good enough to be persecuted much here by the paganism of the most Christian nation in the world. Since most of us are lukewarm, we are therefore safe, for the world persecutes especially great saints and great sinners. Both threaten its comfortable compromises.

Why does the world feel threatened by great sinners? The answer is that not only do they hurt people, but also they expose the world's own evil. Shameless sinners implicitly throw an unanswerable challenge at the world: "Why not be a great sinner, a selfish opportunist, a shameless criminal, if only you can get away with it?"

The world has no answer to that simple question except that we find such an attitude "unacceptable." That is perhaps an interesting fact about the feelings of the speaker, but it is in no sense an answer to the question asked. With no transcendent source of moral authority, no "thou shalt" or "thou shalt not," the world must persecute its criminals not because that is an absolutely right thing to do but because force and threat are its only possible answers to crime and to the fundamental challenge to the world's empty ethics that the criminal poses. "Why not be a criminal if I can get away with it?" The world's only possible answer is: "Because we shall see to it that you don't get away with it." So sinners as well as saints are persecuted by the world. It was fitting that Christ was crucified between two thieves.

Christians in America are not used to being persecuted. Therefore when we do experience a little of it, by the media, for example, we often feel surprise and resentment. This is a naive reaction. If we read the Gospels, we should be surprised by persecution's absence, not by its presence. This surprise and resentment often fuels hatred. We can break the chain of naiveté, surprise, resentment, and hatred at its very first link.

Why is persecution blessed? Not because it is persecution but because it is Christ's. The Body shares in the sufferings of its Head because the Head shares in the sufferings of His Body. Those afflictions are blessed because they bless; they redeem the world; and we can help in this greatest of all tasks. As Saint Paul says, "I now rejoice in my sufferings for you, and fill up in my flesh what is lacking in the afflictions of Christ, for the sake of His body, which is the church" (Col. 1:24).

Socrates discovered part of the eighth beatitude when he taught, "It is more profitable to suffer injustice than to commit it." But Christ goes even farther. He says it is more blessed, more profitable, to suffer injustice and persecution than not to suffer it! It is positively blessed to be persecuted, if it is for righteousness' sake, that is, for Christ's sake (for Christ *is* our righteousness, as Saint Paul says). Our persecutions are not only compensated for, made up for in Heaven, but are also blessed on earth, now. The blessing is like a Christmas present that is opened only in Heaven, but it is given now. The seed flowers in Heaven, but it is planted on earth. What is that seed? What is the great blessing in being persecuted for Christ?

It is the kingdom, the thing Jesus came to preach and to practice, to announce and to create. "Blessed are those who are perse-cuted . . . for theirs is the kingdom. . . ." What's that? Quite simply, Jesus is the king and we are His kingdom. The church is the kingdom of God, and we are the church, the people of God. The blessing, then, the great gift from God to us, the kingdom, is—ourselves! This means our new selves, our true selves, our redeemed and sanctified selves, our selves-in-Christ. Hence the very blows of our persecutors are, in the ironic economy of God's providence, the blows of the chisel that sculpt us into ourselves. The world's very attempts to destroy us help to make us.

This kingdom is the thing that makes poverty, mourning, hun-ger, and persecution blessed. This is the pearl of great price, the one thing necessary. We are wise to give up the whole world for this and fools not to, "for what will it profit a man if he gains the whole world, and loses his own soul?" (Mark 8:36).

If we realized the value of this kingdom, we would laugh at the world's worst threats and persecutions as a millionaire laughs at a scratch on a penny. Saint Theresa says that when we get to Heaven we will look back on the most horribly painful life on earth as no more than one night in an inconvenient hotel. If you find that outrageous, blame Saint Paul, who said exactly the same thing first, in different words: "I consider that the sufferings of this present time are not worthy to be compared with the glory which shall be revealed in us" (Rom. 8:18).

"In *us*"! We are princes and princesses, sons and daughters of the King, heirs of all the infinite divine riches of Heaven. That's why Corrie Ten Boom answered the question, "How can you be so sure your Jesus won't let you slip through his fingers?" by say-ing simply, "Because I *am* one of His fingers." That's why the martyrs die with praises and even jokes on their lips. That's why Saint Paul stuck out his tongue at death itself and taunted, "O death, where is your sting? O Hades, where is your victory?" (1 Cor. 15:55).

The very worst the world can do is kill us, and all that does is send us Home. There is simply nothing left to fear, "neither death nor life, nor angels nor principalities nor powers, nor things present nor things to come, nor height nor depth, nor any other created thing" (Rom. 8:38–39). Even the eight things the world considers the opposite of blessings, the subjects of the Beatitudes, are blessings. In the dying words of the wisest man I ever knew, "It's all grace."

CHAPTER FOURTEEN

In Conclusion:
The Winsomeness of Virtue

Moral traditionalists, who believe in the wisdom of the past, seem to their opponents like drab, dour doomers and damners. But they are not. They are rebels, for in an age of relativism, orthodoxy is the only possible rebellion; and they sing as they fight. They have hope even as they pronounce judgment on our civilization. All the prophets offer hope. The patient is not dead yet.

The patient, Western civilization, may indeed die soon and will certainly die some day, for everything human is mortal. But it need not die now. Though we are sliding towards the abyss, there are footholds on the slippery slope, and we can turn back if only we hold onto them. I have presented fifteen such footholds in this book: the four cardinal moral virtues, the three supernatural theological virtues, and the eight Beatitudes. Unless free will is an illusion, we are free to turn, repent, convert, and turn back the clock which keeps false time. Unless we are victims of our instruments, like Doctor Frankenstein, unless we are slaves of time and masters of morality rather than vice versa, we can return. No flaming sword bars us from this Eden. It has been done before. The history of Israel, eternally history's archetype and beacon, shows numerous examples of national repentance and return to God's favor, even after the most abysmal failures. And God, like the father of the prodigal son, always takes us back.

For these reasons, then, we smile, we traditionalists, we old-fashioned moralists; for we are the rebels and we are the hopeful.

Establishment relativists have no such reasons to smile. In *The Fall*, Camus summarizes them neatly: "I sometimes think of what future historians will say of us. A single sentence will suffice for modern man: he fornicated and read the papers." We traditionalists "read not the *Times*, [we] read the eternities," as Thoreau advises. And we read there the astonishing news that God had decided to make us His bride.

There is a superstition around that is dying and will soon be dead: the superstition that traditional virtue is dull. No. Virtue is winsome. Virtue wins the world. For we cannot change human nature; what God designed cannot be undesigned. Stomachs made for food will always hunger; no stone will ever take the place of bread. The same is true of the stomach of the spirit. The skeptic has the same stomach as the believer, but a different diet. He can't help finding the genuine food filling and fulfilling if he only finds it. He may scorn the beliefs of a Mother Teresa, but he cannot scorn *her,* once he meets her.

They do not know what virtue is. They think it is like prunes: old and wrinkled and awful tasting. They oppose virtue to happiness, thus reversing the oldest and wisest equation of the philosophers, the great discovery of all the moralists, Plato and Aristotle as well as Scripture. They do not see the winsomeness of virtue. This is partly the fault of the defenders of virtue who have bought into the false opposition between virtue and happiness, virtue and joy, virtue and verve, and who have lost the key to the winsomeness of virtue, passion.

The ancients could be passionate about virtue. This strikes us as quaint today. Spencer, in the sixteenth century, could still picture Virtue as a beautiful lady. By the time of Milton, in the seventeenth century, God's virtue seems cold and stern and unlovable, while Satan's vice seems far more interesting. Nietzsche popularizes this contrast: between the "Apollonian," cold and rational and right, and the "Dionysian," fiery and passionate and evil—and interesting. But Hannah Arendt is right when she wrote of "the banality of evil" (in *Eichmann in Jerusalem*); and the Inklings (Lewis, Tolkien, and Williams) have shown that good is far more interesting than evil, though few other writers have.

It is hard for liberals to feel passionate about virtue because they tend to identify with universal issues of social justice, distant and correct. Conservatives identify with local loyalties like family, neighborhood, and marriage, the things you feel irrational passions about.

But we are designed for passion as well as reason. So when the liberal gives us no outlet for our passion in the area of virtue, only in the area of vice, and when the conservative shows a passion for virtue, it is no contest. When the world is shown, as it was two thousand years ago, that heroic virtue is the most fascinating life in the world, the world will be won.

A recent poll of American Catholic teenagers asked what their church was failing to give them that they wanted most. The number one response was: a high and heroic ideal! Teenagers! They may be the salvation of us all.

The stakes are high: survival in this world and happiness in the next. When the players know the stakes are high, they play with passion. When others see passion, they are fascinated.

Why then are most people today not fascinated with virtue? The answer is that most people who practice virtue do not do so with passion. Passion can win the world. The world will be won when Yeats' lines become no longer true:

The best lack all conviction while the worst
Are full of passionate intensity.

An absolute being, an absolute motive, and an absolute hope
can alone generate an absolute passion. God, love and Heaven are
the three greatest sources of passion possible. We are sitting on a
dynamite keg. It exploded once, and changed the world. It can
reignite again. It *must* happen again, because if it does not, there
will be no world to change. Let us save our world, for Heaven's
sake.

A MATTER OF LIFE OR DEATH

There are, then, three reasons to practice virtue, one heavenly
and two earthly. The highest and heavenly reason is to please God,
out of love for God, Who is Love. The second reason is to be
human, to have a healthy human soul. Virtue is soul-health. The
third reason is to survive. In the nuclear age we must love one
another or die. But the third reason will not work without the other
two. For it fails to answer the crucial question *why* to survive, for
what earthly or heavenly end?

It is true, terribly true, that without virtue we will not survive;
that if we do not go back to virtue we will soon return to the jungle
or to the dust. But we cannot survive without a reason to survive,
and this must sooner or later land us in the realm of ultimate reasons, the realm of religion.

I want to prove three principles, which are related logically in a
syllogism:

1. Without virtue, civilization dies.
2. Without religion, virtue dies.
3. Therefore without religion, civilization dies.

In other words:

1. Virtue is necessary for the survival of civilization.
2. And religion is necessary for the survival of virtue.
3. Therefore religion is necessary for the survival of civilization.

The first principle is easy to prove. Just look at history. Each civilization has survived and thrived in proportion to its virtue. It has decayed when its virtue decayed. Israel, Greece, Rome, and the modern West are examples.

The second principle is illuminated by Dostoyevsky's famous saying: "If God does not exist, everything is permissible."

That statement is a corollary of a well-known argument for the existence of God, the moral argument. This argues that because *not* everything is permissible, because conscience speaks with authority, because we know vice is not permitted and virtue is commanded, therefore we know God must exist. Who else could command so absolutely and so authoritatively? Human beings, individual or social, are not absolute. Moral obligation is. Therefore moral obligation cannot come only from human beings.

Nietzsche, that most consistent of atheists, agrees with Dostoyevsky, the Christian, that without God everything becomes permissible. His philosophy calls for a superman who will realize that "God is dead" and thus be freed from moral scruple and guilt. He sees morality as originating in the weakness of the herd and their resentment at this weakness; they invented morality to pull the teeth of the wolves so that they, the sheep, would not be devoured by them. Why should someone who believes this philosophy have moral scruples? Reason gives no answer to this question, and history gives a clear answer. It wears a swastika.

That other consistent modern atheist, Sartre, also agrees with Dostoyevsky's saying. He writes:

> God does not exist and we have to face all the consequences of this. The existentialist is strongly opposed to a certain kind of secular ethics which would like to abolish God with the least possible expense. . . . The existentialist, on the contrary, thinks it very distressing that God does not exist, because all possibility of finding values in a heaven of ideas disappears along with Him; there can be no a priori Good since there is no infinite and perfect consciousness to think it. Nowhere is it written that the Good exists, that we must be honest, that we must not lie; because the fact is, we are on a plane where there are only men.[1]

The hero of Camus' novel *The Plague*, the good agnostic Dr. Rieux, agonizes over the question: Is it possible to be a saint without God? It is at least very difficult. And it is harder for modern man than for ancient pagan man, for modernity is post-Christian, while paganism was pre-Christian.

Paganism was like a virgin, modernity is a divorcee. Pagans are eminently convertible; modernity has already been deconverted. Pagans prize natural piety; modernity scorns it. The pagan exclaims, "Many are the wonders of this world, but none so wonderful as Man!" But the modern is more likely to say, with Oliver Wendell Holmes, "I see no reason for attributing to man a significance different in kind from that which belongs to a baboon or a grain of sand." He is therefore also likely to conclude, with Holmes, that "truth is simply the majority vote of the nation that could lick all the others."

The practical argument for belief in God from the necessity of morality was put nicely by Voltaire when he said, "If God does not exist, it becomes necessary to invent him," and by Chesterton when he said, "If I did not believe in God, I should still want my doctor, my lawyer and my banker to do so."

But this practical argument can be made into a serious theoretical one by asking: How could good morality need false religion? How could goodness rest on a lie? Is the human self so badly split as that?

The issue is scandalously simple. A child can understand it. Sophisticated sophists muddy it with charges of "simplistic" to escape from simple moral obligation. ("Life is always terribly complicated, to someone without principles.") The issue is put to us in all its stark simplicity by Moses, the greatest prophet of the Old Testament, the man who spoke with God face to face. In his last sermon to God's chosen people, just before Moses was about to die and Israel was about to enter the Promised Land, Moses says simply, "Choose life."

The "life" we must choose is first of all God's life, which theologians call "grace," which gives life to our spirits. Secondly, it is the life of virtue, which gives life to our souls. Thirdly, it is the life of peace and of the survival of civilization, which gives life to our bodies. God says of all three together, through His servant Moses:

> This commandment which I command you today, it is not too mysterious for you, nor is it far off. It is not in heaven, that you should say, "Who will ascend into heaven for us and bring it to us, that we may hear it and do it?" Nor is it beyond the sea, that you should say, "Who will go over the sea for us and bring it to us, that we may hear it and do it?" But the word is very near you, in your mouth and in your heart, that you may do it. See, I have set before you today life and good, death and evil. . . . I call heaven and earth as witnesses today against you, that I have set before you life and death, blessing and cursing; therefore choose life, that both you and your descendants may live" (Deut. 30:11–15, 19).

NOTES

Chapter One

1. C. S. Lewis, *The Abolition of Man* (New York: Macmillan, 1943), pp. 87–88.
2. Martin Buber, *I and Thou* (New York: Scribners, 1958), pp. 70–72.

Chapter Five

1. Gabriel Marcel, "On the Ontological Mystery," in *The Philosophy of Existentialism* (New York: Citadel Press, 1956), p. 28.

Chapter Seven

1. C. S. Lewis, *Mere Christianity* (New York: Macmillan, 1943), p. 94.
2. Sören Kierkegaard, "Either/Or," in *A Kierkegaard Anthology*, ed. Robert Bretall (New York: Modern Library, 1946), p. 34.

Chapter Eleven

1. Blaise Pascal, *Pensées*, trans. Krailsheimer (Baltimore: Penguin, 1966), p. 157–159.
2. Kierkegaard, *A Kierkegaard Anthology*, p. 33.

Chapter Fourteen

1. John Paul Sartre, "Existentialism and Humanism" reprinted as *Existentialism and Human Emotions* (New York: Philosophical Library, 1957), pp. 21–22.